So You Want to Sell Cars?

Do It Right!

So You Want to Sell Cars?

Do It Right!

By: John Woullard

Library of Congress Catalog Card Number: 00-191774

ISBN: 978-1-893347-08-3

Copyright © 2008, John Woullard

All rights reserved. No part of this publication may be reproduced, stored in a retrieval system, or transmitted, in any form or by any means, electronic or mechanical, including photocopying, recording, or acquisition by any other form of information recording or storage device, without prior written permission by the Publisher.

MC$_2$ Books is a member of the McGrew Group

First Printing, February 2009

Disclaimer: This publication is designed to provide accurate and authoritative information regarding the subject matter. The author and/or publisher disclaim any and all liability, directly or indirectly, for advice or information presented herein. The author and/or publisher do not assume any responsibility for errors, omissions, or interpretation of the subject matter herein. The opinions expressed in this book are those of the author and not necessarily those of the publisher, booksellers or distributors. Mc^{2}Books are available at special discounts for bulk purchases. Please contact Mc^2 Books, Denver, CO 80231 or call +1 720 220 5097. Find us on the web at http://www.mc2books.com/

Cover designed by McGrewGroup Designs ©2009
Cover photography by Jonathan McGrew © 2009
Inside artwork by Talana Gamah © 2009

Author Contact: Wheelsworth, Inc.
4401 Cottonwood Lakes Blvd.
Thornton, CO 80241
303-920-1419
jwoullard@wheelsworth.net

Acknowledgements

I wish to thank each customer that I have had the good fortune to visit with over the last 24 years. You have been my teachers. I also wish to thank Dave Healy, John Mason, Ron Tetzner, Rusty D'Orazio, Ray McKaig, Paul Ziggenhagen, and Jim Angel. These men were some of the most brilliant people that I ever met in the car business. They shared their knowledge with me and made me a better salesman. I also wish to thank Jon Bradbury for his spiritual advice and his great friendship. Thanks to Geri Estey for helping to brainstorm and compose this work. I must thank Fred Limmel and Larry Bligh for believing in me and encouraging me to continue during the difficult years. Thanks to Karen Reddick, The Red Pen Editor for her discerning eye.

Thanks most of all to my wonderful family. Thanks to Gaye Lorraine Woullard, my wonderful wife, who was all ways there for me as only a wife and friend can be and Clayton Woullard who helped me with this small powerful book and my son Adam Woullard who believed in me without question. Guys, you are the greatest and I love you a bunch.

Contents

Introduction 1
Are You Ready? 5
Employee Turnover 7
Our Different Paths 9
Lay of the Land: Typical Physical Layout 11
    Parking Lot 11
    Customer Seating 12
    Sales Associates' Work Area 13
    The Sales Tower 13
    General Sales Manager's Office 15
    Used Car Manager's Office: The Dealer's Profit Center 16
    Inventory Department 20
    Internet Department 22
    Advertising Department 23
    Finance Department 24
    Clerical Department 25
    Fleet Department 25
    Wash Bay 26
Steps to the Sale 27
    The Meet and Greet 27
        Total Focus 28
        Selling with Emotion 29
        How Do I Deal with No? 30
    Qualification (What Do They Want?) 32
        The Value of Questions 33
        Find the Right Vehicle 34
    Do a Feature/Benefit Presentation 35
        Do a Demonstration (Demo) Test Drive 36
    Go Over Figures: The Write-up 38
    Closing 40
        Assist the Customer to Buy 40
        The Moment of Comfort 41
        Eliminating No as a Possibility 42
        Know When to Be Quiet 44
        The Delivery: Do the Paperwork 46
        No Sale Exit Strategy 52
    Follow-up 53

Prospecting	55
Business Cards	57
Power	59
Increase Power	60
Sales Momentum	61
Avoid Power Drains	61
More on Working Underground	63
Daily Variation	64
Thoughts are Things	65
Honesty and Integrity	66
Success	67
Move Fast	67
Talent, Hard Work and Success	69
Success without Enslavement	71
Goal Setting and Rewarding Success	71
Vacations	73
Your Business within a Business	73
Time Management and Organization	75
Dead Time	75
Daily Book	76
Sales Notebook	76
Balance is Crucial	77
Time Management Aides	77
Product Knowledge	79
Truck Sales	79
SUVs, Vans and Chassis	81
Daily Spiffs	83
Limit the Cash You Carry	87
Referrals	89
How Do You Increase Referral Business?	89
The Value of Using Technology	93
Dress Neatly	95
Do It Right and Do It Now	97
About the Author	99
Glossary	102
Index	107

Introduction

The old man and I had a short but satisfying visit. It was only my second month in the business and I really needed to do well. I had just arrived in the city and spent every dime on attempting to restart my life. Just a couple of weeks prior to meeting this old man I had been sleeping on the floor of a garage apartment belonging to someone who befriended me. After getting my first two paychecks I was able to get my own modest apartment. Now I was sleeping on my own floor. The next paycheck would go toward getting my waterbed.

The old man told me what he wanted. He was looking for a new four-door, six-cylinder automatic. We walked right to it. As we sat down at the negotiation table, he told me this would be a cash deal.

"Fine," I said. I went to check in with my boss.

"What does he want to do?" the silver-haired rascal of a desk manager asked me.

"He is just a tired old man who wants to buy the car. He has not mentioned anything about the price," I told him.

"Well, tell him these cars are in short supply. We will need the full price."

Short supply? We had so many of these suckers we had run out of room.

I had no experience so I simply told this fine old soul what I had been instructed to say. With no hesitation at all, he reached for his checkbook and asked me how much it would be with tax. I gave him a figure and he wrote the check for the full amount. I could picture that waterbed now. I was pretty proud as I walked the deal to the sales tower.

The manager looked at me and said, "What's wrong?" I told him everything was fine and I handed him the completed transaction.

"Just a minute," he said. "You mean he went for it just like that?"

"Yes, he just wants the car and is willing to pay our price."

"Give me that deal," the desk manager said. "You go back and tell him we made a mistake. That car is so rare that we will need another $600."

I returned to the table just as instructed and informed him about the new development. For the first time since we had met, he looked me full in the eyes. Not a word was spoken, but that penetrating look revealed an entire life's story to me. His eyes told me he had lost everyone who ever meant anything to him. He was not a rich man, but had worked all of his days and saved for this time of life. He had denied himself much, but now, in his last days, he was going to have something he had always wanted. The only sound that came from him was a semi disgusted sigh as he turned to a blank page in his checkbook. As he wrote the check, I could not identify the feeling I was having, but I knew it was not good. The deal concluded without incident and I never saw that old man again.

So, this was the car business.

This eye-opening experience revealed as much to me that day as I am sure this book will usher in for you. Who are you? Well, you are someone who wants to make a lot of money. You may be any age, any gender, and have just about any level of education. You are a brave soul and you are willing to give anything a try.

Many of you are wondering if you will have to pawn your soul to the devil to make it in this business. The answer is no. This is just a business. There are many in it that will make it hard for all of us, but it is my hope that many people entering this industry will change it from the inside by practicing honesty and respect while still earning their organizations a decent profit. The intention of this book is to demonstrate how you can be a person of integrity, and at the same time, be a success.

This is an industry where you can make a respectable income if you apply yourself. More importantly, this business needs more competent people running it. I see you as one of those people. You are the future and you can put your mark on this business because soon you will be a force to reckoned with, but for now—let's get you trained!

For many of our customers, dealing with the automobile business ranks right up there with getting a root canal. Your mission is to change that attitude. While this book can give you a head start on making a good living, I hope it also shows that you can do it honestly, and have an outstanding earnings picture. After being a top-selling car salesman for 24 years I can honestly say that I have enjoyed it. I hope that you will too.

Hard work, organization, and consistent practices will bring you a steady paycheck. Luck is always welcomed… Good luck in your new job.

Remember to ***Do It Right!***

Are You Ready?

Are you ready to begin a career in the automobile business? What are your qualifications? What do you need to know? Where can you find the information that will give you a greater chance to succeed? Millions of people worldwide enter this business each year and fail to succeed because of one reason: lack of training.

You, like many of these people, will enter this selling arena because of the lure of big money. The lure is real. A great deal of money can be made without extensive experience. This rare combination of limited experience and good money attracts individuals from a diverse background of careers. Come as you are. Each profession and past job experience only adds to the color and charm of the car business. Charm, however, will not get the job done. You must take training into your own hands. You must take it seriously. This book will prepare you for a great start—but you will need to be your own motivator. Do well!

> *"Profit is the applause you get for taking care of your customers and creating a nurturing environment for your people."*
>
> Ken Blanchard

Employee Turnover

Employee turnover is a huge problem for the automobile business. According to a 2007 article in ***Auto Savant***, a survey indicated the turnover factor in the American automobile industry last year was a whopping 42% (with some years reaching as high as 48%). The national turnover average for all business is only 14.4% according to the Bureau of National Affairs, a news service for professionals. Does this sound like a business you want to be in?

This reminds me of the conversation a dad was having with his daughter who was about to graduate from high school. She was telling him how worried she was about getting a job and/or going to college.

With a big smile on his face and a twinkle in his eye, he said to her, "Honey, you don't have a thing to worry about. You are going to do just fine. As a matter of fact, you are going to knock them dead."

"How can you be so certain?" she asked.

Still smiling in that knowing fatherly way, he said, "I've seen your competition."

The turnover rate in this industry has always been high and continues to be one of the major drains on its productivity.

The turnover rate in this industry has always been high and continues to be one of the major drains on its productivity. It is estimated it costs a company about one-third of a new hire's annual salary to replace an employee. At 14%, that can hurt any company, but at nearly 50%, it can almost decimate an industry or an individual company. One of the big reasons for most stores having this large turnover problem is they consider the car business to be different from other businesses.

The real problem is that if most businesses ran their operations the way an automobile dealer runs his business, there would not be a next year. Poor practices in supervision, stressful situations, dreadful work schedules, ineffective communication and—yes —poor training has caused many dinosaur-style stores to close, sell, or rely on the profitability of their parts, service, or finance departments to keep them going.

> **If you feel good about the place, then go to work for the organization.**

Not all operations are the same. Many progressive dealers put a tremendous effort into hiring the right fit in the first place. They insist on a set training program to introduce the recruit and ongoing education after the hire is made. They also invest in tempting incentives to retain the employee. They promote from within and make all employees aware of career development paths.

These stores actively seek the input of the employees through open-door policies, suggestion boxes, and regular meetings. They utilize sensible work schedules and avoid bell-to-bell days.[1] They will offer a great benefit package that includes medical, dental, life insurance, vacation pay, investment plans, profit-sharing plans, and even retirement plans. These are the dealers we recommend you seek out.

You can learn a great deal on your first interview. Write down the questions you want to ask. Interview more than one store before taking a position. How did the place feel? Did it look clean and orderly? How did the salespeople look? Were they happy? Can you be happy representing the product?

If you feel good about the place, then go to work for the organization. Most turnovers take place within the first ninety days because the employee is not happy about some part of the organization. If you are still employed after ninety days, then stay and give it your best shot.

---

[1] Bell-to-bell refers to a salesperson working the entire day or shift, i.e., 8:00 a.m. to 8:00 p.m.

> *The place where you lose the trail is not necessarily the place where it ends."*
>
> Tom Brown, Jr.

Our Different Paths

The automobile business is filled with people from many walks of life. It follows the true American call of "give me your tired, your poor, your huddled masses yearning to breathe free, the wretched refuse of your teeming shore. Send these, the homeless, tempest tossed to me, I lift my lamp beside the golden door!"[2] The wealth of personalities makes the automobile sales force a truly heterogeneous group. Managers have some challenges due to having to coordinate the different experiences of these individuals.

Your challenge will be to fit in as quickly as possible. Be shrewd—use your previous experience to aid you in this new career. Your customer will not have any objection to hearing a couple of tales from your days as a plumber as long as it is quick, inoffensive, and has something to do with the flow of the deal. Use point of view from your last job to assist you early on in your selling career.

Develop an area of expertise. If you were a tax accountant, use that angle with the small business owner who is considering expanding his fleet. If you were a diesel mechanic in your last job, use that to talk with authority about this area of the automobile business. Let your fellow salespeople know about your expertise and you will get a lot of *turns* from them when they run into trouble with that diesel truck customer. A *turn* is giving your customer to another salesperson for the purpose of increasing the probability of a successful close.

Be a person, be yourself.

Bow to your strengths while picking up as much new material as possible. Do not be concerned about your lack of experience selling automobiles. Be a person, be yourself. Automobile selling experience is

---

[2]From ***The New Colossus*** by Emma Lazarus; posted at the Museum of the Statue of Liberty.

helpful, but <u>people</u> sell automobiles. Be personable and talk with the customer as a fellow person. Learn more about what they do and find common ground. Remember to let them do some of the talking, too.

Even if you decide to only spend a short time in the automobile business, you will probably find it has helped you become a better conversationalist with total strangers. This is an invaluable tool to have in your lifetime toolbox. It is a great experience. My wife is often amazed at how readily I meet people. I can be at a football game standing in line for a beer and a brat and just fall into a conversation with the person behind me. She will usually ask, "How do you know that person?" To which I reply, "I do not." Enjoy the encounters. Be who you are and good things will happen–like a potential customer. You will be able to find common ground earlier and earlier in the transaction.

Another thing your automobile experience will do for you is to give you a great fallback position. If you can learn the trade then you can have a job just about anywhere cars are sold. How many other trades allow you to land in any city in the nation and have almost immediate employment? Since most dealers pay on commission, they will hire you on the spot if you appear to be knowledgeable. All you really need is a pen. Most stores will start brand new people with a modest guaranteed salary for the first few months and many offer programs that pay veteran salespeople a small salary if they fail to bring in a minimum income. In 2008, the average salesperson in the United States earned slightly more than $900 per week.

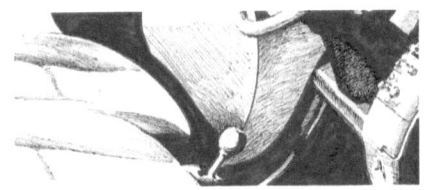

> *"I was seldom able to see an opportunity until it had ceased to be one."*
>
> Mark Twain

Lay of the Land: Typical Physical Layout

On the first day at your new place of employment someone will be assigned to show you around. Pay attention and try to remember where everything is located. Soon you will be in action in each of these areas; learn as much as you can before going live. The typical layout of a dealership will vary from store to store, but what follows will give you enough insight so as to reduce confusion the first couple of days in your new job.

Parking Lot

In many stores, the parking lot is where you will meet the customer. Some stores will tolerate lines of salespeople waiting to rush to the next customer before they get out of their cars. These salespeople are often referred to as *lot lizards*. Chasing after customers is an unprofessional tactic and you are advised to avoid it. Visitors are uncomfortable with this type of initial contact. Work on getting as many appointments as possible so you will not be dependent on floor traffic.

Up system: Each salesperson waits their turn to take a customer.

Low profile system: Each salesperson keeps a low profile, stays widely dispersed and allows customers a time buffer.

Many of the manufacturers are emphasizing a more moderate approach to this initial contact. As a result, some of the stores will use an *up system*. In this type of system, each salesperson waits their turn to take a customer. This is fair to each person; however, it often has a negative effect on those with initiative. This system also requires someone to administer traffic flow and tends to pool the sales force in to more of a holding area. Another effect of this system is that morale becomes worse the longer the group stays huddled together.

Many dealers use a better system. Salespeople are requested to keep a low profile, stay widely dispersed and allow customers a time buffer. The customer is allowed to get out of their car before being approached. The aim is to introduce comfort as early as possible and make your customers feel welcomed. While it is advisable to go easy during the greeting stage of the transaction, waiting too long to acknowledge the prospect can have an obviously negative effect. The right timing has more to do with balance than going to either extreme.

Customer Seating

There are many theories about showroom arrangements. Some stores use tables in the middle of the showroom while others use the semiprivate office approach. Some stores use an approach of plush furniture randomly planted throughout the showroom. Most showrooms are designed to make the customer feel comfortable.

In years past, the showrooms were little more than indoor warehouses. Now there are many Taj Mahals springing up all over with water features, imaginative architecture, expensive flooring, and plush decorations everywhere you look.

The showroom is where you and your customer may meet. Most showrooms house shiny new automobiles and offices for sales and management. During inclement weather you may find it easier to do many steps of the sale here before you venture outside. Practice professional etiquette and keep the area spotless.

The sales floor is under constant supervision by management. In many large stores, there is a floor manager, closer, or a team leader. Their job is to ensure control of customer activity. They will look to see if customers are being attended to, if the flow of the sale is going well and/or to keep the customers from leaving before the boss has a chance to talk.

Sales Associates' Work Area

If you are fortunate enough to have a desk, then organize it the first or second day you are on the job. Do not depend on anyone else to help you. Go out and buy your own folders and filing materials. If the drawers are filled with junk, take all the junk out and put back only what you can use in the very near future. An organized area will save you a great deal of time, and time is money.
(See *Time Management and Organization*)

The Sales Tower

Most operations make use of a control room or sales tower. This is the area where you take your sales proposal. A veteran manager instructs you on how to proceed. The desk/tower manager has a wealth of information and experience. He is aware of prevailing market conditions, the owner's desired business direction, and he is also able to inspire and encourage those working on his shift. This individual will be your real-world trainer. Whatever you have picked up by reading this book will be tested and put to work by your tower manager. You will want to gain as much knowledge as possible from this person and filter out what does not work for you.

> **Loading the salesman's lip:** Telling the salesman word-for-word what he is to say to his prospect

The sales tower is not a good place to hang out; keep this area open for business. Most tower managers will find something for you to do if they think you are being unproductive. Some dealerships hide this function while others use it as a tool to coerce and marshal behavior. All sales go through this facet of the operation, so get to know as much as possible about the people who man it.

On my first day on the job I noticed a very large man sitting at the sales tower. He seemed to possess the area like a great bald eagle perched on his nest. Observing just a little longer I saw a salesman present an offer. The huge head of this man peered over the edge of the sales tower and from behind a set of steamed glasses his eyes pierced that poor slob while a wealth of profanity poured forth from his lips. Later it was explained to me that he was *loading the salesman's lip* (this means telling the salesman word for word what he is to say to his prospect). One thing was for sure, he had that guy's attention.

When my turn came to face this fire-breathing dragon I decided to stand tall and hold my ground. Being 6'8" helped just a little bit. The great head rocked back and forth as if he were sizing up a prized bull, and while those penetrating eyes softened just a bit, I was on guard for anything. I presented my written proposal without saying a word. As he checked me out again I noticed a slight smile on his face as he wrote the note that I was to present to my customer. All of my senses told me that he was feeling me out. I knew that my response would set the tone for our relationship.

Without a word he turned the offer sheet around for me to read. Instinctively I took the page, turned around and headed to the table where my customer was seated and did not look at the sheet until I was seated with him. Now as I read word for word what he had written I fully expected for the customer to get up and leave. Instead the man asked me if this guy was nuts. His offer to the customer was $2,000 more than the vehicle had listed for at full price. I was to learn later on that this tower manager had done two things: he fully intended to evoke emotion, and he was also attempting to get the customer's thinking up. Had I lost control of the customer, there was a floor manager stationed close by ready to play good cop if the customer decided to leave.

tabling a deal: You are required to bring your proposal to the sales tower in a specific manner

My customer and I visited for a while and he made a reasonable counter offer. When I re-presented the offer, this giant man began to talk in a slightly demeaning manner; again I exchanged no words with him and took his offer without looking. We later became good pals and he told me that playing blind poker with him on that deal earned me a lot of respect in his eyes. Each situation will require your best judgment, but do not worry. Your job is to learn as much as possible from each selling opportunity.

Each manager has a different personality and learning how to communicate with each person is important. Present your transaction in a businesslike manner and in written form as often as possible. At peak times, this manager may be working several deals. He will be better able to assist you if he can see the written information rather than trying to remember the verbiage from each person. Every dealership has a formal preference for how to *table a deal*. (Tabling a deal means you are required to bring your proposal to the desk in a specific manner.) Some variations might include:

1. Having the deal in writing *before* handing it in.

2. Bringing an earnest money deposit with your deal.

3. Taking in a written trade appraisal.

4. Requiring signatures on your offer.

Each dealership will add its own wrinkle.

Sales tower etiquette can take many forms and each person manning the tower has his own set of requirements. Get a feel for each person you work with and work with that person accordingly. Sometimes you can get your feelings hurt if you make a mistake. Many times you may get the deal turned to another person if you are not working it to the tower manager's specifications.

Part of the tower activity may involve another person who reviews the arrival and departure of each customer. One of the many names for this person is the *sales hawk*. His job is to see that all customers are waited on in a timely manner. He or she will also require all salespeople to account for what happened with the customer.

Management will not allow for you to *burn through ups* (working with a large number of ups who never buy or even drive a vehicle). The function of the sales hawk changes from dealer to dealer, but it is important for you to know that someone is watching. Use this as a positive and see this person as a part of the operation rather than someone who is out to get you.

General Sales Manager's Office

The office of the General Sales Manager (GSM) will always be close to the sales floor. The GSM is very important to the total dealership's success. This key individual reports to the owner or a general manager. The obvious duty of the GSM is to generate sales. This manager will know your name early on and will be one of the people who will be keeping an eye on your progress. You may have already met this person because they often are involved in the hiring process.

The GSM is responsible for sales and profits in the new and used car department. He will often serve as your desk/tower manager. He is also in charge of the finance department. Other duties of the GSM include holding weekly sales meetings, sales planning and forecast, inventory replenishment, assisting with advertising, handling customer complaints, auditing other managers, sales staffing, and compensation planning.

The GSM normally starts his career as a salesperson and usually has a couple of years of experience before being considered for this position. A high school diploma is the minimum educational requirement. In 2008 the salary range spans $90,000 to $160,000 per year. This salary range can be on the low side in larger outfits. You are only a couple of years away from this job if you are interested and can prove yourself.

Used Car Manager's Office: The Dealer's Profit Center

Many dealerships have combined the new and used car showrooms, but other dealerships still employ a separate facility. It will be very important to give yourself a tour of the used car department if no one offers to show you around. **Make sure you are ready to do business** and that you know where everything is.

> **Customers have no problem pawning off a lemon on the dealer.**

The used car manager is important to your success. He appraises trades and purchases inventory from wholesalers, private parties, auctions, and other sources. This person will also be responsible for merchandising stock and preventing the stock from getting old. His responsibilities also include reconditioning, pricing, and marking down the inventory.

When you have finished your demonstration of the used (or new) vehicle, be sure to return it to its spot. This is important so that other people will not have to look for it while you and your party discuss it. Also, it demonstrates control and is a silent indicator to your customer that someone else may want it just as much as he does. If you have noted any problems or deficiencies on your demonstration ride, please give a written note to any manager so the problem may be resolved.

You will need to bring all your trades to the used car manager. This manager is a very mobile person and finding him or her can be frustrating when you need a trade-in appraised. If possible, get his cell phone number in order to track him down. The appraisal card is your responsibility—you need to fill it out completely.

In the heat of the battle, you may skip steps because you want the deal. It is good the deal matters to you, but control starts with how well you pace yourself. If you cannot slow it down enough to get control of yourself, then this same lack of control will show up throughout your deal and you will blow a lot of money, and probably your job. Take care of the details.

> **Your appraiser will also look for cleanliness on the inside of the vehicle.**

A complete appraisal card helps the experienced used car manager determine a number of things and is just the beginning of a complete evaluation of your customer's trade-in. Items such as an out-of-area address can indicate the car could have been driven in a location using a lot of salts on the roads or could have been involved in a flood. The appraisal may show hail damage or, in many cases, the vehicle may have been in an accident. Most problems usually involve a bad transmission or engine concerns. Customers have no problem pawning off a lemon on the dealer, but they would never dream of selling the same car to a friend or even someone out of the newspapers. You may be surprised with what revelations your used car guy comes up with, but your customer will very seldom be surprised.

Many times I have walked back to the negotiation table and asked customers if they have received their insurance check for the hail damage. They will usually say yes. There are a few who will honestly not know about the hail. Often small hail does not leave big dents, but the damage is just as real. In these cases, customers can still make an insurance claim and still trade the vehicle in. Most of the time, they will be grateful you helped them with the problem.

Your appraiser will also look for cleanliness on the inside of the vehicle. A cluttered and dirty vehicle will indicate the rest of the unit has most likely not been maintained correctly either. If you are aware that your customer will be arriving with a trade-in, tell them to get a wash job and to remove everything from it except the owner's guide. This will help increase the value. The appraiser will also look at the brake and gas pedals and the condition of the driver's seat. If he detects a lot of wear in these areas, he will know it was driven in the city more than on the open road. As you know, it takes a lot more out of a car when it's driven during stop-and-go traffic. He will also look for mismatched tires, door, trunk and hood fit, paint match, and an array of minor items.

He will give you the Actual Cash Value (A.C.V.) of the vehicle. You will not be allowed to tell the customer what this number is unless your desk manager approves. If your customer is trading in a vehicle on a fully marked-up used car, the desk manager will show an allowance equivalent to the A.C.V. plus the amount for which they are willing to discount the new car.

In the following example, the trade-in has an A.C.V. of $1,500 and the unit the customer desires has a $4,000 mark-up. If the value of the marked-up unit is discounted by $2,500, the customer will be told that their trade-in is worth $4,000 (discount of $2,500 + A.C.V. of $1,500 = trade allowance of $4,000). The reason why the dealer uses this practice is because most of your customers will remember what they paid for their trade and will feel that it should be worth more than it truly is. Again, the inflated value of the trade is called the trade-in allowance and is a combination of the A.C.V. plus discounts from the unit your customer is interested in purchasing from you.

When presenting the value to your customer, be careful not to demean his trade. For many people, this has been a reliable old friend that has brought them through many storms. There is often a sentimental value attached that has nothing to do with the car's real value.

Remember to always work for your customers—your customers must feel that you are on their side. If the trade becomes a problem, then you may be asked to kick it. (*Kicking the trade* means you advise customers that the deal may go better if their trade is not included.) If the car is old and has little value, then you might suggest your customers give it to a family member, a charity, or their church. Many churches and other organizations will accept these gifts and your customer can do better by writing the unit off as a tax deductible item. Do not represent yourself as an expert in that regard, unless, of course, you have a solid background in accounting or tax law. Instead you may suggest they consult their accountant or tax professional for advice.

If the trade is a more recent model and has a payoff, then you may employ another tactic. Show your customers they are really getting more for their trade than it appears. In an example where the offer is $20,000 for the trade, you may show the customers that by leaving the trade in the deal, they will enjoy the tax benefit. If the customer lives in an 8% tax area, the trade is really worth $21,600, if left in the deal. Since the entire deal will be taxed on the trade difference, then they will pick up another $1,600 by leaving the trade in the deal. Observe how the deal works with the trade left in:

New Car Cost	$ 30,000
Trade is worth	<u>20,000</u>
Difference	$ 10,000
Tax at 8%	<u>800</u>
TOTAL	$10,800

Now observe how the deal looks when the trade is withdrawn:

New Car Cost	$ 30,000
Tax at 8%	<u>2,400</u>
TOTAL	$ 32,400

The difference between deals is:

Taxes paid on no trade	$ 2,400
Taxes paid on trade-in	<u>800</u>
Difference	$ 1,600

States allow this practice because the trade-in has already been taxed once when it was purchased. Your customers will not have to pay tax on it again. If they believe they can sell it themselves and make a better deal, then their buyer will need to pay them more than the $21,600 they are getting from your generous dealership.

You might also remind them that when the car is traded to the dealer they will not have strange people coming to their home, they will not have advertising expenses, nor will they need to be concerned about their buyer's ability to borrow, and they will not be responsible for things like the lemon law or having to fix the unit if it breaks down shortly after they sell it. You are offering them a trouble-free deal where the paperwork, the payoff, and all the other details will be taken care of by your very professional title department.

If all of this fails, you may ask the tower manager if he can put more money into the trade. Many times the manager may know of another party who has a burning desire for the trade. If your customer's trade is from a competing brand, your manager may phone that store's used car manager, give him a description of what you have and ask him if he would like to buy it. He may make a better offer because he may have better traffic and more people looking for that particular used vehicle. If he makes a good offer, you and your customer could come to an agreement.

If you cannot agree, then offer to help the customer sell it himself by looking up the book value, helping write the ad, and even offer to field questions any potential buyers may have. Stay involved in the deal, if it makes sense. If your store has a consignment policy, you can seek permission to put it on your lot. Make the deal!

Inventory Department

In larger stores, the inventory is manned by a full-time individual. This person's responsibilities include ordering regular stock, promotional stock, handling dealer trades, customer orders, and ridding the stock of old and problem merchandise. In smaller stores, this individual may have additional duties.

Do not give your customer room to say no.

No store will have every item you need. The inventory manager can help you make dealer trades for units you do not have. One caution here: many times management will warn you to sell what is in stock. Clear it with management before utilizing this tactic.

Your inventory manager will have a working relationship with many other stores who sell your brand. He will often be able to pick up the phone, and in a matter of a few moments, have an arrangement worked out with another dealer. In many cases, the exchange can be made the same day and your customer will think your dealership is on top of its game.

The inventory manager will also know about merchandise that is in transit to your store. Many times I was delighted to know the truck or car I needed was sitting at the train yard waiting to come to our store. A good inventory manager will also be able to inform you about units that are being built for your store. Sometimes, your customer will wait.

If all else fails, suggest a factory order. A tip here is *not* to ask your customer if you can order the unit for them. Do not give your customer room to say no. Before you go back to your guess, give your inventory manager a sketch of what you know about the customer's wants and needs. Have your inventory manager work up an order and print it out for you. Have your tower manager set the price of this item in writing. Show the printed version to your client and make it simple, short and sweet.

The effect is often amazing.

First of all, the potential order is in writing. Next, the customer has to like it because it has his colors, the seats, the engine, and transmission all at a great low price. It effectively takes the person out of the market. Waiving the order deposit is a great way of getting a commitment from your prospect. Even if he leaves your store without making a decision, your competition will be fighting to find your customer's dream vehicle that you have already offered to order.

If your store is extremely aggressive, and they feel this is the type of merchandise they should always stock, then you can request they order it for stock. You may now follow-up with your customers, apologize for not having it in stock, advise them you have ordered it for stock and that you would like to offer them the first right of refusal. Ask them if you can bring it by for them to see when it arrives. This works better than you may believe.

Lastly, the inventory manager will probably know if the vehicle you need is out of the store on a demo ride, at a showing in the mall, having accessories added, being repaired, being driven by the owner's wife, or any other number of crazy reasons. Be sure not to wear out your welcome using this approach. You are employed to sell what the dealer can deliver today. Balance your decision. The inventory sitting on the lot is costing a fortune and the pressure to move it is squarely sitting on many shoulders. You will probably share in this feeling of pressure. Make the deal and get on to the next one.

Internet Department

The typical layout of a modern dealership will include an area where computer-literate personnel communicate with customers who are seeking information, via the Internet, to purchase an automobile. Most dealers are associated with buying services that assist people in getting the best price. The customer is normally referred to a dealer who is near his residence.

Skater: **Someone who tries to steal another salesperson's customer**

The Internet sales personnel verify pricing and in-stock condition. The sales department then sets an appointment to deliver or show the automobile to the member. As a new salesperson, you will be in competition with this department. They operate on a smaller profit margin than you will be allowed to work on; however, in some states, they will authorize you to show the customer around.

When you greet a customer for the first time, it is always a good idea to ask them who they are coming in to see. This will save you many wasted hours of working someone else's customer. It is also important to not give other professional salespeople the impression you are trying to cut in on their transaction. If you get branded as a *skater* (someone who tries to steal another salesperson's customer), then you will create many enemies early on in your experience. That is not a good thing.

According to Nancy Stracione, Internet Sales Director for the Fred Beans Family of Dealerships in Pennsylvania in a ***Dealer ADvantage*** article on Cars.com, "more than 80% of all people looking to buy a new car will do some research online."[3] This area of the business will continue to grow. If you have an interest, this could be a career path you may want to investigate. There are very few stores without their own website and Internet department. Ads are appearing daily for Internet sales personnel and a whole industry is forming to train these people.

One national site, AutoTrader.com, says it provides access to more than 1.5 million used cars. Tech-savvy search engines are easy to talk to in everyday language and these sites provide additional information that buyers relish. Hundreds of dealers are spending a great deal of resources on their own sites and are also using dozens of other sites to get the word out. The Internet manager will instruct you as to how to work the deal.

Advertising Department

In most stores, this function is controlled by the GSM. In larger stores and in multiple brand stores, there will probably be one single person who handles this program.

Their job responsibilities focus on creating traffic to the dealership. A great deal of care is taken in creating the proper phraseology. There are legal regulations that each dealer must follow, but they do get near the edge on these advertisements. Most stores use all media avenues, including newspaper, radio, television, Internet, glass print, electronic billboard, still billboard, bench advertising, sports teams, airplane banners, local organizations, and on and on.

It is a full-time job in many organizations. Advertising can be the salvation of a dealer. The dealer depends heavily on the sales force to greet and handle customers responding to these ads. Most of the time, there will be a meeting prior to running these ads. The discussion in these meetings will generally include inventory quantities, tactics to sell related items, ad-on sales, floor coverage, spiff (cash awards paid on the spot to the sales team), commissions, finance options, and a host of other areas of concern. You will be shown how the dealership wants you to respond to questions related to the ad.

---

[3]http://dealeradvantage.cars.com/da/2008/05/dealer-profile-2/

Finance Department

This manager is called by many names. Some stores call him the F & I manager, finance manager, the business manager, box manager, or finance director.

The finance department is a real profit contributor to almost any operation. It is usually positioned for privacy from the sales floor. Most finance departments will consist of a series of offices manned by one or more managers. Most stores will require all customers go through this function regardless of whether they are paying cash, doing outside financing, or seeking dealer financing. The finance director and/or his managers will work closely with all customers. These key people will usually meet with you before they talk with your customers. They will make sure your paperwork is in order and enter it all in the computer. When the customer has completed their business in the finance office, the manager will let you know and then you can finish the delivery.

The best idea is to stay available while your customer is in the finance office. Your F & I person will make attempts to sell their products. Some of their products include finance rates, extended warranties, credit life, disability insurance, gap insurance, appearance protection, wheel and tire programs, and window etchings. Some of your customers may have had experienced something similar to this before. They may be ready to leave by now. There is usually little trouble settling them down.

Since this process can take up precious selling moments, you will need to take steps toward reducing time for all involved in the process. Some things you can do are to set your appointments for slow days and times. If you are working a phone customer, you can get a credit application filled out before they arrive. If you know the car they want, you can have most of your paperwork filled out, and if you know the price you will be selling this car at, then you can have everything filled out before they arrive and simply have them sign in the highlighted areas.

Cover everything you can with your floor and F & I manager prior to your customer's arrival. If your customer is unexpected, have all of your paperwork carried as far as you can. During high peak sales times, your F & I manager may recommend setting an appointment at another time. It is his call. Be available when your people are with the F & I manager.

Clerical Department

The dealer's clerical office is where most of the records are found. Functions such as payroll, title processing, on-order files, accounts payable and accounts receivable, and other clerical issues are located in this office. Salespeople are usually restricted from this area. Managers will have freer access. These people usually have a great deal of specialized experience. They may not always have the overview. They will work for an office manager who is a key person in the everyday working of the dealership. This person is the second best person to start with after your team leader.

Fleet Department

The Fleet Department is a part of the sales effort responsible for selling larger quantities of merchandise to businesses and other big-time organizations. The concept of fleet sales is based on giving customers a larger discount if they are buying large quantities or if they buy often. Government sales and special purchases (having to do with *body building*) usually go through the fleet department. *Body building* refers to installing a specialized bed or some other special operation on chassis cabs and van frames. If the customer needs a dump truck, a lift basket, flatbed, stake body, or some other technical operation, the fleet department will usually get the call. City governments also will order their equipment from a fleet salesperson. Most government business is done on a bid basis. The buyer will send out a written or faxed invitation to bid. Their specification sheets are very detailed and will generally have a time deadline.

In many operations, the fleet department and the Internet department are separate. Other stores may have one or the other. The general emphasis of fleet sales is centered on repeat commercial customers and quantity buyers, but there is no clear line between the two departments.

The fleet business is generally divided into three categories that are differentiated by volume:

1. The small fleet owner will have between one and four vehicles and generally will be around zero to two percent over factory invoice.

2. Those fleets having between five to 14 units receive pricing in the invoice area and may receive special rebates.

3. This third group of businesses will have 15 or more units. These businesses will usually receive merchandise below invoice and are often given additional rewards direct from the factory.

Fleet personnel will likely have had plenty of experience working with different programs that apply to these specialized customers. Many stores demand these customers work with no one other than the more experienced fleet people.

Wash Bay

Your vehicle will go to the wash bay where your prep team will remove packing slips, wash the exterior, clean the interior, and make the unit available for departure. It is your responsibility to make sure the job has been done right before your customer sees their brand new vehicle. First impressions are unforgettable.

This department is in charge of receiving the new merchandise, getting it to service for its mechanical inspection, preparing it for display, maintaining it each day of its dealership stay, and finally preparing it for its new owners. These are the people you seldom see, so treat them well. They can really make a difference in your delivery.

> *"Nobody's a natural. You work hard to get good and then work hard to get better."*
>
> NHL star Paul Coffey

Steps to the Sale

The Meet and Greet

Someone once described the meet and greet as "the first moment you experience when you walk into a cold shower." That first instance is shocking, but the shock quickly wears off. All you have to do is endure the pain through the first few seconds. When you meet your customer for the first time, you are setting the tone for the rest of the transaction.

A number of things happen during the greeting. Both salesperson and customer are making evaluations: How is he dressed? What about the eye contact? Is he walking away from me? Is he smiling? Will he shake my hand? In truth, the greeting started when you got out of bed this morning. You woke up fresh—or with a hangover. You had a good start—or you did not. You had a great drive to work—or you got a ticket!

Your customer had the same kind of morning and now you are about to meet. Should you have a canned speech? You can have a couple of favorite lines but remember that no two situations are the same. You should **practice being spontaneous.** If Mom and Dad have their six-year-old daughter tagging along, comment on how lovely her hair ribbon looks, or compliment the beautiful paint job on the teenager's raised pickup truck. Do not miss an opportunity to compliment.

Here are some basic things to remember:

- ✓ Create comfort
- ✓ Say less and ask more
- ✓ Respect the other person's personal space
- ✓ Reasonably match personality traits

Now, let the party begin. Is your first question about the weather? An introduction? Will it be new or used? Or, can help them find someone? It is a dance. Have fun with your customers. Make yourself comfortable and they will be comfortable also. People buy during a moment of comfort. Seek to really help them and it will all be OK.

Total Focus

Some things should be obvious, but allow me to mention here that you should drop everything when your customer comes in. Nothing infuriated me more than to see a salesman finish his conversation with another party while his customer stood without being acknowledged. Turn the cell phone off or put it on vibrate. When your pals come up to chat with you, tell them you will get with them in a little while.

If you are fortunate to have two customers at the same time, make sure to put customer number one on hold, acknowledge the second person (briefly), and make sure you have made an arrangement that will serve both parties comfortably. One way to avoid this type of collision is to make an appointment and space each one out so you can handle all comers. As you gain more and more experience, you will have no trouble working three or more deals, if need be, at the same time.

Focus becomes a factor that you can use to cut the sale time down. If you can reduce the time factor, then both you and your customer will be fresher at the end of the deal. Cutting the average four hours down to two is a challenge for many houses. In the fleet business, just a few moments of face-to-face time is required in some deals. Reducing the time in the deal is important to your overall productivity and improves your overall popularity with your customers.

Another thing that will help your meet and greet is to be prepared. Always be ready for your customer's approach. Have a pen and a backup pen with you and something to write on, and please do not ask for permission to finish your cigarette. A real warm smile should be automatic. Make them feel at home.

Selling with Emotion

One of the best salesmen I know is consistent in how he greets both his first time customers and his lifetime repeat customers. Not only does he have a smile on his face, but he laughs as well. People feel like they are coming home. His extended hand is hard to resist. He treats his customers like royalty and he makes sure he never appears to be superior to them. He is genuine in making them feel he is in their corner. His grosses are amazing and his repeat and referral business is tremendous. His greetings create emotions and he knows that if there is no emotion, there is usually no sale. People love to be entertained and they love to hear stories. When you do your active listening, encourage your customer to tell you a story about a point he is inclined to ignore. Get into the flow and drop in an interesting story of your own.

Emotion is everything!

Emotions have played a part in getting your party into the showroom. There was the interest generated by the television ad, there was the excitement generated when they saw the neighbor's new car. They were delighted when that new car passed them on the road, their feelings were reinforced when questioning the lady at the gas station regarding the fuel economy, and they will be overwhelmed at the demonstration ride that you are about to give them. Emotion is everything!

We have all heard the expression, "Sell the sizzle, not the steak." That expression first appeared in the 1930s and is attributed to Elmer Wheeler. Wheeler explained, "It is the sizzle that sells the steak and not the cow, although the cow is, of course, mighty important." Our cow is a beautiful, brand new automobile. There are so many improvements, so many grand specifications, so many new facts and solutions involved with our product until we feel obligated to spend time sharing all of this rational information with our customers. It is fair to note some of this is necessary but, as in all things, balance is absolutely important. The great chef uses just the right amount of salt—too much salt and the meal is ruined.

People buy ideas. You are a master artist. You must paint a picture for them. Don't sell them a bundle of firewood; sell them a quiet evening with the kids hanging out in front of the fireplace with marshmallows being toasted to perfection while he and his wife smile affectionately at each other. Blend your benefits with the features and remember a benefit is not just what a feature will do for your customers—a benefit is an opportunity to tell a very short story.

People like stories as long as they are short and good. These mini-tales have the effect of making your customers more comfortable. The more often you can push their emotional "hot buttons" by using your mental transporter, the more often you will close deals. **All deals are a series of short closes**. These short closes are not a request for the customer to buy. These closes put their fears and concerns to rest. The best close is no close at all. When the presentation is done properly, the outcome is just a thing of beauty and the deal closes itself.

How Do I Deal with No?

Do not set the stage for it. Do not expect to hear no and do not ask questions that can only be answered with no. Share control with your guests. When your customers tell you "no," do not take it personally. In the game of selling, they just helped you narrow the possibilities. Do not pretend that you did not hear them, do not sidestep the objection, but do not overemphasize the problem either. Make as brief a reply as possible and move on if they will let you move on.

Proxemics: The study of the nature and degree of the spatial separation individuals naturally maintain

The standard situation of asking customers if you can help them generally results in the reply, "no, just looking." What do you do? Briefly go in the direction they wish to go (which may be away from them), then turn and give them what they want. They really want to look and get help from you *if they need it*. Your silent assistance will be appreciated while you let them browse.

Giving space is important. You do not want to be too close or too far away. Do not violate their personal area of comfort. The personal area of space can be anything and will depend upon the individual. A great deal of study has been done in this area. The science is known as *proxemics*[4]. It is defined as the study of the nature and degree of the spatial

---

[4]Hall, Edward T. (1966). *The Hidden Dimension*. Anchor Books.

separation individuals naturally maintain (as in various social and interpersonal situations) and of how this separation relates to environmental and cultural factors. Anthropologist Edward T. Hall states: "Personal space can be viewed as an extension of the human body." He further states these areas can be viewed in four distinct zones:

1. The Intimate Zone: for whispering and embracing (within 18 inches of your body)

2. The Personal Zone: for conversing with close friends (18 inches to four feet)

3. The Social Zone: for conversing with acquaintances (four to 12 feet)

4. The Public Zone: for interacting with strangers (12 to 25 feet)

These zones vary from the guy who grew up on a farm to the guy who grew up riding the subway. Women have a closer zone of comfort and protect space to the side of themselves while men will want more space and will protect space directly in front of them. People from other cultures might also stand closer or farther away than you're used to. Before you offer your help, you will need to identify your potential customer's tone and pace. If the tone is loud and quick, you will want to take that information in and match it without imitating them.

Now you offer the help they are unwilling to admit they need by using observation to break the ice. If they are looking at used cars, you may start with: "Most of the used cars are here, but the freshest arrivals are in the rear, or the pricing codes are on the windshield on the driver's side."

From here you are good to go to the next stage of the sale. Now start by giving your name. If your prospect extends his hand or offers his name, then you accommodate him. If he is interested in seeing the new arrival, then you take the lead and he will follow. Let the good karma flow and proceed onto the next step of the sale.

Qualification (What Do They Want?)

The second stage of the sale known as the qualification stage. A lot of things happen during this stage. The main idea of this stage is to find out exactly what they are looking for, but this is also where you decide to go all the way with this transaction or decide if you want to work a turn for the sake of putting another person in who has a better chance of closing the deal.

A good rule to remember is not to insult anyone.

What seems to be the person's **hot button**? Do they really know what they want? If so, will they share it with you? If they do not know what they want then use questions such as: Car or truck? New or used? Two-door or four-door? Stick or automatic? Foreign or domestic?

Why don't people really know what they want? Because this is life's biggest impulse purchase and there are so many choices. At every traffic light, most people lean over and ask, "What kind of car is that?" I bet you are doing the same thing. My wife is constantly asking me if I know the make and model of an automobile. Here I am, the great automobile guru, and I have no clue.

About 10 years ago, there were more than 600 new models available to the public; last year there were more than 1,300 reported models available to the buying public. This complexity of models with all their variations makes it difficult even for a veteran car person. So how can your customers really know what they want?

A good rule to remember is not to insult anyone. Your customers may not know what they want, but you had better not let that become a problem. Set up the "right vibes" at the beginning. Help the customer make the right purchase. Don't worry about the profit. Most people like good service and will tip for it. Your tip will usually be a larger commission and a great referral. But do not make him feel intimidated.

The Value of Questions

During the qualification stage, the rule is questions, questions, and more questions. While there are no dumb questions, there are many unasked questions. The reason you want to qualify your prospect early is to save time. Why is it that this is one of the places where the sales process most often breaks down? One reason is because only five minutes ago you met this person for the first time. You have been trying to get to know them and establish a rapport. In essence, you are juggling two balls here.

Allow time for a clean and clear response.

As you change from the greeting to the qualification stage, you will need to consider using a transitional element. For me it was a tone of voice. When my tone changed from: "It really has been nice getting to know you and I hope you like me also," to: "Now I really want to help you find your perfect vehicle," the customer instinctively knew it. I used a slight change of tone that was a little harder and a bit more serious. Your prospect has been expecting this change and the only thing you need to do is avoid going on too long in the greeting mode.

When you ask the why, when, what, which, where, how, and who questions, please allow time for a clean and clear response. This is called *pace* and it begins to set the tone for the closing table. There you will ask a question and the first one to speak loses. You also want to be sure you are listening effectively and you do not have to ask for a repeat. What are your prospect's needs? Who is the decision maker? When will he need it? Where will he use it? Other "w" words such as will, which, and why will help trigger your memory so the sale stays on course.

Another keyword is *how*?

How much are you willing to spend, or what is your budget are key questions. When this is done effectively, you will not waste three hours only to find that Mr. Prospect cannot afford the vehicle you landed him on. While you do not want to be specific, you can offer a range of pricing. Let your prospect know when he is out of his comfort zone of pricing. Politely ask him if he has decided to spend more money. Keep him focused on what he is willing to spend.

Find the Right Vehicle

I was rather amazed one day when a very disgruntled man sprang out of his car and headed for the lot. When I approached him, he had no trouble letting me know what he wanted.

"I want a car that has the brake pedal the same height as the gas pedal. I really do not care what brand it might be," he said.

I had never heard this requirement before. I was dumbfounded. I just had to know why this was so important. He explained he had just got into a car accident because his foot got caught on the side of the brake pedal as he was transferring it from the gas pedal. It was very difficult for me not to recommend that if he had not been following so close he would have had more time to react.

During your time with the customer, a small change begins to take place. You slowly start taking control of the transaction. Most of the time, there will be no objection to this because most customers are out of their element and what they are really looking for is someone they are able to trust and who they feel will not skin them alive.

In order to know the right vehicle, you will need to ask questions. Most people will be concerned about the money you will offer for their trade or the bottom line for the new vehicle, but 80% of the time it is about the monthly payment. When you ask about the monthly payment, most will give you something lower than what they are willing to pay.

At this time in the transaction, you may explain the $5,000 rule:

For each $5,000 of the vehicle you are buying, your payment will be approximately $100 per month.

This often helps your customer to begin qualifying themselves. How accurate is this rule? It is accurate enough!

Resist the temptation to get too deep into the figures at this stage of the game. An old adage in the automobile business is to "talk figures on your seat, not on your feet."

If the decision maker is present, then proceed to the next step if everything is going well. By going well, I mean each person must be in agreement. Be sure to probe for acceptance of all parties.

In family situations, find out who the decision maker is, and do not assume it is the husband. Many times we make the mistake of assuming that one member of the household is the decision maker. While some surveys suggest that women influence 80% of the buying decisions on vehicles, both influence the outcome of the sale.

If the decision maker is not present, then devise a plan to get that person involved before you go too far on the targeted vehicle.

If the situation lends itself, suggest driving by the location of the missing decision maker to show that person the vehicle on the demonstration ride. If the sale has a better chance of closing without you being there, then seek to put your customer in a borrowed car agreement. Most dealerships will make a limited use of this procedure. Upper management will usually have to approve such an arrangement. Sometimes a simple phone call can solve the problem.

In the case where the woman is doing the leg work, avoid the appearance of indicating she needs someone else's approval to close the deal. In many cases, she earns more than he does and in many cases there is no "him" at all. Be careful not to step on any toes.

In business situations when the decision maker is not available, the drive-by or phone call may be all you need. Since most business decisions are based more on previous planning than on impulse buying, then the decision has already taken place regarding this purchase. In most of these cases, it is a matter of price and specification being met.

Your job, in either case, is to get the information early in the sale as to who the decision maker will be. Again, use tact and touch in obtaining this data.

Do a Feature/Benefit Presentation

In our earlier discussion on selling with emotion, we covered the notion of "selling the sizzle." As we review that area again, take note that the purpose of a feature/benefit presentation is to explain what the vehicle can do and then translate that into how it will benefit your potential buyer. The trick is to know how much to talk. This type of presentation can be made lengthy by presenting the entire vehicle or just by concentrating on the hot buttons. Do not oversell the vehicle and do not undersell the unit.

You may wish to switch to another vehicle for any number of reasons. Avoid the *absolute trap*. As you present different items, avoid making statements that trap you. Do not attempt to force your taste on the prospect. An example is: "I hate four-door cars; here, let me show you this nice two-door hatch." Alas, you now find out that the four-door is exactly what his daughter wants. Reversing course is very difficult and definitely takes the wind out of your sails.

Most automobile transactions last four to six hours; people get tired and want simply to get away to recuperate. A good goal for duration is two to three hours. You are in control. You can and must exercise control over the length of the deal. Your closing percentage will increase and you will have more time to work additional deals for more income.

Do a Demonstration (Demo) Test Drive

The demo ride is highly emphasized in most organizations. Many managers believe the best salesperson on the payroll is the automobile itself. They will often inform their sales force to "let the car sell itself." There is a lot of truth in that statement. The drive does another thing for the customer and the dealer: it creates emotion. It does not matter how well you perform your job. If you have not interjected emotion into the transaction, then there is very little chance you will get a quality close.

How do you get your customer to take the demo drive? First of all, do not anticipate a problem. If you begin to think about a problem, it will come across in your voice. Remember that thoughts are things and they take on a life of their own the more attention (negative or positive) you give to them. Second, do not ask the customer to take the ride. Take control. Do your exterior presentation, take your position behind the steering wheel and present the features and benefits of the interior.

If your prospect is peering over your shoulder, ask him to come around and sit down beside you. If another party is with him ask them to get in the backseat and also look at the dash presentation. Begin the dash presentation at the driver's side and systematically go across.

Never let them drive first.

Finally, crank the unit; turn on the air conditioner, radio, etc. When you are done with your dash presentation, instruct your prospect to close the door because you want to demonstrate the ride quality. Never let them drive first. Always have two planned routes. One route should be the long route and the other should be a shorter route. Remember to buckle up.

A good demo route should include high-speed roads, regular highways, streets, railroad crossings, and a few places to change drivers. Seek out a high-speed highway as early as possible. When getting onto a high-speed interstate, demonstrate the ability of the car to safely accelerate to highway speed. This maneuver will also evoke emotion. After you are on the interstate, demonstrate the one-second lane change. Be careful your vehicle is not too top heavy, but the reason you are demonstrating this is to show the customer how the unit performs in an emergency maneuver. Again, this just might bring out a whoa! And possibly even a giggle or two.

Pull up near a big rig and roll the windows down, and then roll them up again so they may experience the quietness of the vehicle. On a slight incline, step on the accelerator and experience the climbing ability of the vehicle. Put the car through its paces and give your customer a good show. Do these motion exercises early. Now, lock on the cruise and chat with your customer as you relax for a while.

Always tell them what you are going to do before you do it. As you approach your changeover spot, inform them you are going to demonstrate a controlled panic stop. Make sure you have practiced this move before you go live with your customer as a lot of emotion will be added, as a matter of fact, your customer will probably be glad to get you out of the driver's seat. At this point in the ride, I remember one of my customers telling me he was impressed with the car and he did intend to buy one from me, just not this one. We all had a good laugh.

When you change seats, be sure to adjust the seat and have your customer adjust the mirrors. Take them back to the dealership on a different road. Make sure to let everyone drive. Have the customer park and get them comfortably seated inside the showroom.

Go Over Figures: The Write-up

Shall we look at some figures? Would you like to see the bottom line on this one? Let me show you the new discounts on this one. These are all sayings you can use when the time comes to close the transaction or find out why they're not buying. Fortune favors the bold. Step right up and pose any question that comes to mind. Just do it. Suggest that you can have it ready in 30 minutes. Are you ready?

One of the things you must believe in is the sticker price of your vehicle.

This is the point in the transaction where many new salespeople and most customers will begin to dread what is to follow. Now it is time for the negotiation. Have you ever asked yourself why this is required? When you were at the grocery store, there was no negotiation. When you were at the dental office, the doctor's office, the pet store, or the floral shop, there was no negotiation.

What about something large? That new home you just purchased, did you ask to see the invoice on it? Did you ask to see a copy of the invoice when you bought the $5,000 big screen television or the $10,000 diamond ring? You probably did not. But everyone wants to know what your dealer paid for this shiny new hybrid. The problem exists because we taught people to negotiate with us. As you know, it began with the horse and buggy and continues now.

One of the things you must believe in is the sticker price of your vehicle. At least two or three times before you get into the heat of the battle, you should simply restate the asking price somewhere in your conversation. If the truth be known, in some base-priced units, there is very little markup and even with the dealer's holdback award, it is hardly worth him selling it.

There are other ways of starting the negotiation for the automobile. Many dealerships begin with a discounted price, which they call a no-haggle price. The theory is that by reducing the list price, the customer will feel no need to ask for more. Other dealers will use the list price plus an additional amount that they may call a market adjustment. This is usually a vehicle that is in very high demand.

Another often-used tactic is to start at list price and ask for an offer. Other approaches start with an exaggerated option that the dealer claims to have added. The customer has to first challenge these additions and after that he is less likely to ask for more discounts.

Most transactions will generally come down to money down and monthly payments. Dealers are more than happy to deal with these items because financing is where most dealers really make their money. Most formats here begin with an old, and favorite, method called four squares. A sheet of plain paper is generally divided into four equal parts with the following words:

1. Trade
2. Purchase Price
3. Down Payment
4. Monthly Payment

Here is how it works. The salesperson will draw a four-quartered square:

Trade	Purchase Price
Down Payment	Monthly Payment

The figures for your customer's trade will be lower than what the dealer is really willing to pay for the trade; the purchase price will be as high as the dealer dares to raise it; the down payment will be much more than it needs to be and the monthly payment will be inflated.

In this system, the salesperson will observe the area that the customer objects to most. Then the salesperson asks if that area of the deal were changed to the customer's satisfaction would he purchase the vehicle. This is little more than the old shell game. The salesperson continues to write down their desires, gets them to initial the offer, and takes the offer to the manager to get what is usually a compromise reply. After several compromises, the deal is then made.

The closing method is very effective, but if your idea of selling is to trick or push people into doing things, then you will find your vehicle returns to be very high and your referrals will be low.

This business is about helping people do something they really want to do, but they do not want to be taken advantage of while doing it. But can you make a good profit while being honest with your customer? Yes, most often people will agree to a fair price, but fair can mean many things.

Closing

Assist the Customer to Buy

Closing the deal can be done in different ways. The desire of our institute is to make it a business transaction in which everyone wins. The people you sit across from will help you with your business *if* you will simply treat them right. What does "treating them right" mean? It means setting up a winning situation for dealer and customer

---
Good customer treatment also means that you put them in the right car.

The biggest question sales associates fear is if they are open and honest, will they produce an acceptable profit for the dealer? One of the first things you will learn in this business is your biggest profits will be made from your happiest customers. Happy customers will return again and again and send you untold referrals. If you have done the job right you can expect a good profit. You will also get good marks on those new automobile surveys that are becoming so important.

On the other hand, the worst customer you will ever have is the one who fights you for every dime. You will encounter this type of customer 20% of the time. They will ask for a couple tanks of gas, a set of floor mats, or a free oil change. They never finish being a pain. Their referrals will also be mooches. Fortunately this type of customer constitutes a limited but painful few. For most of your customers, the lowest price is not the *main* concern.

Good customer treatment also means that you put them in the right car. As you become more and more proficient at your occupation, you will learn to listen effectively and have a strong idea of what your customer is saying and not saying. Sometimes you have to dig a little, but in the end, everything will be fine and you will not be one of those salespeople who takes a car back on Monday morning because it did not fit the customer's needs.

It is especially important to fill the right order when dealing with trucks (See the Section on **Truck Sales** on page 88). Most people will be dealing with towing needs, cargo volume, or payload factors. If you are not sure, then seek out a proficient sales partner to assist you. It will not take long before you develop enough expertise to help these types of customers, and they will enjoy their purchase for years to come.

The Moment of Comfort

People buy during a moment of comfort. Your task is to keep them smiling and nodding. On Dave's first day, he shared with me his uneasiness about being in sales. He said he had no idea of what to say or where to begin. I asked him if he had any problem sitting in his living room talking to his best friend.

"Well no," he said, "but that is different."

When I asked him why that was different, he told me they had known each other for years and they shared a lot of values.

"I can tell old Jim anything," he said.

"Dave, from this day forward every customer is Jim," I said as I reached to shake his hand.

Selling is just having a conversation. Feelings are always involved whether we are aware of it or not, but that is a good thing. Salesmanship involves taking feelings into consideration while you plan your closing strategy.

Listen to yourself. Did you just change your tone of voice because you are in a selling situation? Allow yourself to be natural and comfortable. As you participate in the exchange, be aware of what makes you feel better. If you are doing fine with those thoughts and feelings, then it is probably being picked up on by your customer. Again, be natural. You are a fine person and you are participating in a very noble profession. Salespeople make the world go round. Every item you look at right now was sold by someone. Most of us are salespeople at one time or another. Your job is to sell automobiles.

One of the best tools a salesperson can possess is plain old silence. You do not always have to speak. Active listening is part of the performance. You listen for tone, you check out body language, you allow the other guy to talk so as to build trust and comfort.

Your goal is to create a winning situation for all parties. In order to achieve this goal, it will be necessary to set up a condition in which the customer recognizes this is not just about him. Your organization also has to be represented. Your employer has a huge investment and is providing a fine combination of services for the public. Lightly touch on this one. You do not want to create an *us-against-you* attitude; your job is really to be a friend to customers. They must be convinced you are on their side. If you have a closer or a person acting in a higher authority role, then he will explain the company's position. Let the manager be the bad guy—you are the customer's friend.

When it is obvious the deal is ready for inking, you should spare no time with chit-chat. Get a verbal agreement, if needed, and seal the deal with ink. It is much easier to close a deal when the foundation work has been done properly. When a doctor has performed a brilliant surgery, then closing comes as a natural part of the operation. It is the same way in sales. No good doctor would remove an organ and then let the patient lie around. No great salesperson would have done everything perfectly and then wait for the customer to close themselves. It is all about timing and the time has come to close. Just do it!

Eliminating "No" as a Possibility

No one wants to hear the word *no*. You are now in possession of very important information. Be sure you do not use the word no anywhere in your presentation. So how do you find out what you need to know from your prospect to advance the sale? Use open-ended questions. An open-ended question is one that cannot be answered with a yes or no. Some examples might be: How are you going to use your truck? How much weight will you be towing? How many passengers will you be carrying?

Keep a selling diary

Become armed with another piece of essential information: you and your prospect have an idea of where this entire process is heading. You know you will sell something and you know your prospect will buy something. There is no safe haven in assuming that it might or could not happen. Paint a no-stressed picture of success in your mind and advance the sale in the right direction. Smile and act as if both your objectives were already achieved. Take small steps and inform your prospect about what you will do next. Do not ask permission if it can be avoided. Listen carefully for the place where the customer might bring up an objection and supply them with an energetic viewpoint before they voice an opinion. Anticipating the customer's objections becomes easier with time. A pre-emptive strike is always advisable: Sir, I realize this unit exceeds your budget, but I think you are showing good judgment in reassessing your plan.

Control is a very important factor in sales and you should always be in control.

You will not sell everyone, but you can learn from each transaction. As your career progresses, you will learn more and your closing ratio will improve. However, this does not happen by accident. One key is to keep a selling diary. At the end of each day, make a couple of notes about what you have learned. Look at it like a self-review. My goal was to make seven out of 10 decisions correctly, but never repeat the three errors I made. What is your goal?

Remember, that *no* is not the end of the road.

Another key in dealing with no is to read the customer's emotional state by checking into your own status. This is actually very easy. When you feel the knot in your gut (a sure sign the deal is not going well), then you can bet the other guy is doing the same thing. Your job is to provide that moment of comfort. Change the subject, tell a joke, make a turn or excuse yourself for a moment. The customer does not have to know what you are doing. Go comb your hair, check your appearance, compose yourself and reenter the situation refreshed. Now you both feel a little better. Remember, that *no* is not the end of the road. It is only a warning sign informing you of an upcoming situation that you will have to react to.

Know When to Be Quiet

One of the first things many beginning sales people learn is when to be quiet in a negotiation. Timing can be everything. On the other side of the table or desk, you are dealing with people who are not confident about what is going on. They are on your turf. They often do not know what a good deal is, what they can really afford, and how much money you are making off the deal, and a wealth of other factors often adds to their uncertainty. If you are to be trusted then you must first make them comfortable and reduce their uncertainty. They will also be looking for a consistent story. If they detect deceit, you will lose that element of trust. That is why you must do everything in your power to avoid the lies.

When you have made your presentation, you will have to decide between two roads. One road will be to ask them to make an offer and the other will be to inform them of what you will accept for the automobile. Whatever you do, there is always one constant rule you should observe:

Shut Up!

The first negotiator to speak will be considered the loser. Know when to be quiet. Allow them the opportunity to say yes. Act as if you expect their answer to be yes. Regardless of what the answer is, be prepared to respond slowly. Do not have a mental response prepared beforehand. Let your response be spontaneous and tailored to the moment. Assume the close. Finish your paperwork and deliver the car.

Turns

A *turn* is giving your customer to another professional for the purpose of increasing the probability of a successful close. When a turn is made, the deal is split between the first person and the one who actually makes the close. In stores that employ a great deal of new people (often new, inexperienced people are called *green peas*); the turn is done quite frequently.

Do not say one word unless you are prompted to do so by the *turn person*.

Usually, the floor manager will decide who will be the *turn person*. Many times the manager will use a more experienced salesperson to make the turn. You may be told to introduce this individual as your manager, the truck manager, the used car manager, or anything that presents authority. If you are a truthful person, you may find this as a moment of conscious struggle. My experience shows that lies weaken the car deal. I usually try to come up with an introduction I could live with, such as: Mr. Customer, our management feels that Mr. Jones here can be helpful in advancing this deal.

If you are involved in a deal at the closing stage, make your introduction; and, if you are invited to sit in, make sure you observe one extreme basic rule: **Do not say one word unless you are prompted to do so by the *turn person*.** Speaking out of turn can get you fired on the spot!

Most houses recognize when the turn is made that each of the two people are then *married*. This means if the deal concludes successfully, each party gets half of the commission, and if the first person on the deal takes a new customer while the second person is closing the deal, then the second person is entitled to half of
each deal.

To avoid being married, a salesperson may request a *complete-out* turn. This means the person taking the turn will receive the total commission if the deal is concluded successfully.

Wait, it gets better!

If the marriage is in effect, and a second person is unable to close the deal, and a third commissioned person is brought in to close the deal, then the rule states that the middle person is out. The commission will then be split between the first and the third commissioned salesperson.

There are always exceptions to every rule. Usually the manager will make the decision in most stores as to how the deal is to be commissioned. In some stores, management will allow the matter to go to arbitration. The members of the arbitration committee usually will be fellow salespeople. This group will listen to both stories and make a decision they will present to management.

Tips

I was stunned one day when a customer I worked with earlier returned to see me. I asked if he had returned to buy the vehicle to which he replied, "No." He informed me he had purchased elsewhere, but had been so inspired by my presentation that he just wanted to buy me lunch. After he handed me a $50 bill, he said he would have gladly purchased from my store, but we just did not have the vehicle he wanted.

The next time you are dining at a fine establishment, notice how your waiter moves around you and your party. What is it about this person that makes you leave a nice tip as opposed to a small one? When you are in a selling situation, your customer is making the same observations about you. He may not leave you a tip as he would at a dining establishment, but you will often be rewarded if he feels you are going out of your way to help him. Do not do any phony stuff he can see through, but figure in a full tank of gas, or a set of floor mats, or ski racks, or just the right little touch, such as having him meet the owner.

The Delivery: Do the Paperwork

There was one store I worked where I was still in training class and we were not supposed to have customer contact, yet our training coordinator wanted us to get the feel for the Saturday business. While standing near a truck, a customer approached me and there were no veteran sales people around. He asked me the price of the truck; I looked at the coded price and told him what it was. He said, "That's what the other guy told me, but I did not believe him. I would never buy from him anyway, but I will buy it from you." I had no idea of how to fill out the paper work, but I found a guy who was not busy and asked if I could pay him to help me with paperwork. He agreed and I presented the full price offer to the sales tower; they liked me right away. They agreed my training was now over.

Congratulations! You have made your first deal. Your manager tells you to do your paperwork. The next phase of the transaction is where a lot of income can be lost. To get a sense of what I want to convey, I want you to remember the most successful time you have ever had fishing. One thing that will be common to most experiences is you wanted to catch as many fish as you could while they were biting. Many times in your selling career you will experience these feeding frenzies. Amazing as it may sound, more than once I have seen two different sets of customers wanting to buy the same car; the car had been on the lot for weeks with very little activity. Who knows what causes these quirks in people? Selling highs come and go, and you want to be prepared as well as you can be when opportunity knocks. Here is where good training and preparation pays off.

First of all, there are only so many forms you will ever need to complete your deal. In many houses you will see the sales representative looking for the right one or two pieces of paper. He knows that he is burning valuable selling time, but has not caught on to the fact that preparation is one of the major keys to selling success.

Resist the temptation to take a break.

Prevent this problem by making up several folders containing all the forms you will need beforehand. Look at each form and determine what you can sign or initial before you are engaged in your prime time selling hours. Use your highlighter to underscore where your next customer will be signing. This forces you to anticipate and visualize the next closing. This type of mental energy can assist in activating the law of attraction. Put these folders away and set up a backup stash of forms.

Also, have available a small tool box that you can lock. Stock it with:

- ✓ a screwdriver
- ✓ a crescent wrench
- ✓ pliers
- ✓ extra nuts and bolts

- ✓ a razor blade
- ✓ a tape measure
- ✓ a small flashlight
- ✓ a cordless drill (buy one if you have to)

You will become the draw of the sales floor after a short time. Your fellow salespeople will ask to borrow your tools. Do not do it. Inform them you do not loan tools and just don't do it. If you do, you may get your tools back the first time, but you will never see them again most of the time. Lock your box and hide it. All of these little things add to your sense of preparation. Preparation helps erase doubt and fear and increases your quotient of confidence, and confidence closes more deals.

Now that the deal has been accepted by both parties, your customer will want to get going ASAP. Most dealerships will want you to get your customers to the finance office. On busy days, you will get stuck waiting in line with your customer. Many enlightened houses will dispatch backup personnel to assist with this portion of the transaction thus freeing you up to sell more merchandise; however, a majority will tie you up because they have always done it this way. The idea of increased productivity at heavy volume periods has never dawned on them.

In the old dinosaur stores, you will also be required to make the delivery and say good-bye. Too bad you can't use the turn here. How long did it take you to complete the sale? You must know so you can improve in this area.

Resist the temptation to take a break, get a smoke, go out for food, or any of the many things non-pros do. If the store brings in food at high volume times, then get a bite and get back to work. Prepare for all the food to be gone by bringing enough food to get you through or have a file folder of food delivery places on hand. Take a short visit to the restroom, check your appearance and get back to work. The best time to sell another vehicle is when you have just sold one. At this time you are just about bulletproof. Take your next customer with the attitude that you are about to do him the biggest favor of his life.

Financing

Most people who purchase a new automobile will need to make payments. As a beginning salesperson, you will need to keep that in mind when you are qualifying your customer. Many times you will hear a person ask if you have merchandise that may end up in the $30,000 range. You can spend several hours coming up with something your customer is happy with, get to the closing table and then find out the $600 payment is a great deal more than your customer wants or may be able to qualify for. As noted before, a good guideline when trying to put your prospect on the right car is:

$5,000 of car = about $100 per month of payment

This rule can be influenced by rate and length of months to pay off the unit. This rule is based on single-digit rates for approximately 60-month loans.

Also, keep in mind that taxes are a factor if your prospect intends to finance them in. Most of your prospects know they can finance the entire purchase amount with nothing down. It will be your job to get as much down payment as possible. Money down equals greater profit margins for you and the dealer. Also, the more down, the more the prospect will like the final payment.

When asking for money down, a good lead line is: Will you be making the usual 20% down? You may explain that banks typically ask for 20% down so they can be in an equity position. Because automobiles depreciate 15% immediately and taxes are at least 5%, banks request this ratio on moderate credit risk. You may then mentally let the prospect off the hook by indicating you are sure his credit is better than most.

You may also ask: Will your down payment offset the taxes or do you wish to finance them as well? Quite often the customer will at least ask you how much the taxes will be. This is a good line of questioning because it does get more money down and it also causes your prospect to think about taking possession of the vehicle.

Lease

The automobile lease business has grown considerably over the last three decades. When your customer leases the vehicle, he will only pay for a portion of the vehicle's total value and the customer will keep the vehicle for only an agreed upon length of time. During this lease period, the customer will be responsible for maintaining the unit just as if they were buying it.

It seems each spring I get a customer who comes in with an easy-to-read expression on their face. I was having a lot of fun with this charming lady who had just become an empty nester. I knew even before she said it, she wanted a red convertible sports car. "How did you know?" she said. I had to admit we had seen the pattern often during this time of year. These empty nesters have done their duty to family and now it was their turn.

I recommended leasing a new car rather than buying a used one. I also recommended she take a short term 24-month lease. I did not want to curb her enthusiasm, but explained after 24 months she might want to drive something else. National statistics show the repossession rate spikes heavily around the 24-month level. People become bored at this time and want something else. Many who have the means will suffer through one more year and trade at about 37 months. She took my advice and I am sure she had 24 months of fun reliving her lost youth.

> **The amount of value left at the end of this period of time is called *residual*.**

People lease for many reasons. Most people are looking for a lower payment. Others will want to get more upgrades for their automobile budget dollar. Before pitching a lease, be sure to clear it with your management team. Not all cars lease well and your manager will advise you which are good candidates.

Leasing has many other advantages for your prospect. Leasing allows the customer to drive a new car that is under the manufacturer's warranty and allows the customer trouble-free driving. It also reduces the typical parts replacement period that a long-term owner suffers through. This period begins with the first set of tires, then brakes, shocks, exhaust, etc. These expenses often are referred to as hidden costs because they happen at different intervals during the ownership period without accumulative recognition. They can often amount to several thousands of dollars.

Leases also allow for sales tax to be paid monthly. A customer buying a $30,000 automobile and living in a 9 percent tax area will immediately pay $2,700 of taxes.

If an individual finances the purchase, he will also pay interest on the taxes. Even if he only keeps the vehicle for a short time, he is still out a ton of money and the vehicle has also depreciated every month. The person who leases a vehicle is making a $500 monthly payment and will pay 9 percent of $500 for a total of $545 per month. If he holds the vehicle for a couple of years, his tax payout is $1,080 versus the buyer's $2,700.

Leasing allows the customer a painless exit at the end of the ownership period because the customer does not have to worry about selling or trading in the car. There is also the possibility of selling the leased vehicle at the time of termination and making some money.

The profile for a lease candidate is a person who keeps the car for two or three years. Their annual driving is usually between 10,000 to 15,000 miles. Ask your prospect to tell you about the last three automobiles they owned. How long did they retain each automobile? How many of the cars were new? Write down each fact given because putting it in print will have a more resounding consequence. When you have all the data on paper average the time Mr. Prospect keeps the vehicle. People are often surprised to find that they are keeping vehicles shorter periods of time than they realized.

Again your short term prospects should definitely consider the lease. If at least one of the cars was new then there is further evidence that a lease would work well for your customer. There are other leases with more time and more miles, but drivers who can keep the lease miles under the manufacturer's warranty will have the best results. When working with these clients, your manager will calculate the lease terms and direct you as to how to present it to them. Some words you will need to know about are *residual, cap cost reduction, security deposit, lease time period,* and *money cost*.

The automobile will depreciate over time. The amount of value left at the end of this period of time is called *residual*. This value can be expressed in either percent or dollar values. A $20,000 Manufacturer Suggested Retail Price (MSRP) vehicle with a 60% residual will be worth $12,000 at the lease's end. Vehicles holding their value are better to lease because part of what is paid for in the lease payment is the depreciation. *Cap cost reduction* is down payment. The *security deposit* is an amount of money the prospect will have to leave until he brings the vehicle back at the end of the lease. The *lease period* is the length the lease will run and money cost is finance charges.

One of the major objections to leasing is a very solid belief regarding ownership. This misconception begins with their home. Most people's largest ever investment is their home. A common held belief is it is better to purchase a home than to rent it. Many of these homeowners will apply this same logic to their second largest purchase: the automobile. When you explain that these two properties differ in one major manner: property goes up in value, while vehicles go down. A $40,000 home purchased 20 years ago will have more than tripled in value while an automobile will be worth less than one-tenth of its original value. Many are discovering again that it is better to lease what depreciates and buy what appreciates.

While leasing may make sense, it may just not be comfortable for your prospect. Where does your pitch stop? You must take the read. Is it better to win the argument and lose the sale or do what your senses tell you and close the deal with a purchase?

No Sale Exit Strategy

Many dealerships require their salespeople have a manager say goodbye before the customer leaves. If you are employed in one of those organizations, expect very harsh treatment if you let your customer walk. Many times customers are looking for parts or service. If you speak with them for any length of time at all, you will be required to explain what happened.

If your sell has gone through the entire process and there was no sale, then the manager will decide how to put the customer out. The usual manner to exit the customer is to thank him for his visit, and present a manager who will take a final crack at getting his business. This approach is used by stores who work the *be back system*. This strategy is a good one because many people do return, but most old timers in the business will stress never believing customers who promise to come back.

Stores who torture the customers will have a lot of pop-ups and walkouts. Their comments and actions do elicit a great deal of emotion, but not always the good kind. In this type of store, you may find yourself running after the customer trying to make an offer that will bring them back inside. Management in this type of house will insist you never give the customer anything in writing and the reason for this is they do **not** want a written deal that the customer can present to one of their competitors.

My recommendation is you should find a place that will allow you to have a business-like presentation, work your own deal (after a probationary period) and let the customer out in the same fashion in which you would like to be handled. If you have done a good job, then you can expect good results in a high percentage of situations. Remember, this is a numbers game and you will not get everyone, but you will sell enough to make a fine living.

Follow-up

Take the curse off the sale by calling the customer the next day to see if he is having any problems. Many people will still be thinking about the deal and wondering if they made the right decision. This call can help put them at ease before the small doubts grow into larger ones.

Within a couple of days, send them a thank you card. Always include two business cards—do not use one or three cards. Two allows for more than one person to take possession of your cards. It gives you a better chance for your customer to contact you again. Three cards is overkill and lessen the importance of all the cards. This is also a great time to ask them to refer a customer to you. Do not offer to pay for referrals. If you have done your job right, your customer will help you because they appreciated your help, but if the dealership offers a program for rewarding referrals, then you want to put heavy stress on that issue.

"Sales are contingent upon the attitude of the salesman—not the attitude of the prospect."
W. Clement Stone

Prospecting

While you're waiting on your referrals to start coming through, you want to start the prospecting process. In the car business prospecting is the act of hunting for the customer instead of waiting for them to come to us.

For me, the most effective prospecting was to contact my sold customers. These were the people who already showed their approval of me. If they held me in high esteem the first time, why would they not like me once more? My goal was to mail something to these people three or four times a year (I always sent a Christmas card).

> **The average individual will have between 250 to 300 people in their sphere of influence.**

As I already discussed, since turnover in this business is so high customers do not really expect to find their favorite salesperson still employed when they return for their next car. Staying in touch with your customer assures you of being the first one they will call when their next automobile need arises. Frequent mailings also help you maintain a link with them in the event that they move. Even if they move out of state, continue to mail to them. When the change of address information comes back to you, update your computer file. Keep in touch—your customer will be impressed that you care and also that you are a conscientious business person.

The average American family owns between two to three cars. The one that you just sold them will probably be one of the two more that they will need to buy. If you have been in the business for a short time you can see how important it is to let your customer know where you are employed. In addition to their own needs your prospect will be happy to refer more business to you.

The average individual will have between 250 to 300 people in their sphere of influence. You may not think that you know that many people but you do. Review and write down all of the people in your address book. A family of five will count as five contacts if they can be regarded as potential drivers. Check all the numbers in your cell phone, Blackberry, or PDA. Review your e-mail addresses.

Make a list of family members, friends, acquaintances, neighbors, old schoolmates, old employee associates, church members, bridge or other club members; those who provide services for you, stock brokers, doctors, lawyers, mechanics, etc. How many more can you add?

Sales is a numbers game. Almost everyone that you mail or call will have one thing in common: they will own a car. I can almost guarantee you that in the next year you will be having a conversation with someone who will say to you, "Oh, we just bought a car. I wish I had known that you were in the business." Get ahead of this conversation. Write their names down, mail to them, and follow up with a phone call. Salespeople all over the world do this. Why should you be any different?

When you mail to your prospect, realize that your mail will be in competition with all the other correspondences in their mailbox. Make it short and sweet. Whatever your message's content, you are really saying, "I am still here and I absolutely wish to sell you a car." Your customer will appreciate your brevity. Check, double check, and triple check your spelling and grammar. Whenever possible use a pre-stamped postcard that you can purchase from the post office. This will cut in half the number of steps needed to send an otherwise enveloped, typed message.

Be sure to include a return address so your database can be updated if some are returned as unable to forward. Make an extra effort to follow up with these lost customers. Your computer provides some wonderful tools for doing this. One example is AnyWho.com which allows you to enter the customer's name into the search and the service finds the customer's last phone number and address. You can also use the reverse phone number look-up feature (if you suspect your prospect kept their old number) to look up their latest address.

If you are not handy with this sort of thing then hire it out. This is worth tens of thousands of dollars to you. Many of your dealers will handle the expense and mailing if you initiate and oversee the project.

A great moneymaker is the magnet. Have some magnets made to look similar to your business card. Magnets are inexpensive and your prospect will always be able to locate it on the refrigerator. It is amazing how many times I hear my customers tell me that the magnet came in handy.

Another great source for prospects is sitting in the file cabinets of your service department. Some of these records could even be on computer. Each time your customer brings their unit in, these files are updated. They hold a wealth of information in them and have never been used by the sales department in most cases. Most service managers will not want everyone in those files but I learned early that I could pay the clerical person (who normally works these files) if my manager cleared it for me. I would pay her a very good rate to come in on her time off and develop a mailing list. This is a great way for a *green pea* to start a prospect file.

Because the turnover rate is so high you can also take over files from salespeople who are no longer employed. These files are often called orphaned owners. These customers have shown loyalty to the dealer and you can help them by having them come back as welcomed guests. Introduce yourself; send a magnet or business card, and keep in touch.

Calling usually brings about positive results. Make sure to be aware of the no call rules in your state. Do not be afraid to contact these customers. Know what you want to say. It is best to have a written script. You should vary your script based on the customer, but the written script is a good place to start. Do not rely on it, however, and do not make it sound as if you are reading. Sound upbeat and have some enthusiasm for the job that you are doing. Know that you are providing a great service and assume that the customer is always glad to hear from you. **Be courteous**.

Business Cards

Hand out business cards whenever possible. Be selective though. Make a connection with your party. How many times have you been at a gathering where people were handing out business cards and later when you emptied your pockets you had no memory of who the person was? Plant a seed of thought when you **allow** them to possess your contact information. When they take your card it should be as if you are doing them a favor. If you have done the exchange correctly you should hear the person say "thank you." Always make eye contact when making the exchange and be just the slightest bit hesitant when making the handoff.

Give two cards every time.

Another prospecting tactic involves a buying list. Lists are available for sale all over the Internet. It is best to target your list only for areas that you serve. You may also buy lists from county and state governments and other local entities.

There is no substitute for a living person in front of you who wishes to do business today, but if you wish to be really successful, you can help yourself by prospecting.

"He who controls others may be powerful, but he who has mastered himself is mightier still."
Lao Tzu

Power

Power is force. Force can be used for constructive or destructive ends. Make sure you are using your power in a non-conflicting manner. It is easier to push a stone downhill than uphill. Use your power to create. This good life is yours and you have a right to it. The proper use of personal power requires consistency. When you follow your own non-offensive rules, then you can operate with conscious and deliberate actions all the time. Set goals and be clear about what you want. Review your goals daily. Be a self-starter and do not broadcast what you are doing. This tactic builds power and focuses on intent.

While power may be the engine for your boat, intention is your rudder.

Your power and intention work together or they do not work at all. Be sure you do recognize your ability to be creative. Intention is the real motive behind all your action. Believe in yourself.

Power is the ability to make choices and influence outcomes. Now that you are aware of your power and you know how to direct it, what do you do next? Manage the situation. Life sends curve balls, fastballs, strikes and other surprises. That is what makes it life. If it was all scripted and we knew what was coming next, then what fun would that be? On the other hand, we do have a responsibility to anticipate factors that can be divisive to our desired ends.

As a power manager, you will learn from past events. You will learn from others. You will keep up with your business by reading and training. You will learn that whatever you focus on will grow and what you give no attention to will diminish. You will learn how to improve your focus through active visualization. Visualization means seeing or picturing an event. When applying this technique to future events, it has the tendency to help you end up with what you have focused on many times.

Athletes were among the first to employ this art form. The pole vaulter kneeling with his head bowed is probably not praying, he is visualizing the blood flowing easily through his trained body, seeing and feeling the acceleration of his body down the lane, the absolutely perfect plant of the pole, the practiced form of the liftoff, the lighter than air feeling of his body, the ease of clearing the bar, the perfect kick back of the pole, the ever so graceful landing, the smile that is on his face, the feeling of joy in his heart, and the bouncing up to the applause of the crowd as he raises his clenched fist in victory above his head. He sees all of this before he even attempts the feat. He adds feelings to the vision as well. He has practiced this process hundreds of times. He is ready.

Again, this process has been employed in many areas of life and now comes to the business world and specifically to the selling arena. There are many works written now by professional trainers on this subject. The ability to use this power can transform your life. Learn more about visualization and the law of attraction. There are many books, CDs, and websites on the subject.

Increase Power

Rise early after a good night's rest and immediately read something positive, and sit and meditate or just be still and visualize your day. Have a good breakfast and do some exercise. Just taking a walk or a bike ride is enough. If you are an evening person, do your workouts then. Two or three times a week is a good start. During your work day, get in a few minutes walking and try to quiet your mind as much as possible. Recite daily affirmations. They help you hold in mind what you want to see materialized in reality.

Avoid toxic personalities as much as possible. From day one, display this positive behavior and you will avoid those who want to complain to anyone who will listen. Go to work with a plan of action. Know what you want to accomplish and go straight at it. You will probably discover traffic to be slow in the first hours of the day. After lunch, there will be more people to talk with. Make those "slow hours" work for you by making your calls, walking the inventory, and catching up on your paperwork. Always keep an eye out for a customer no one else is working with.

Avoid conversations that involve comparing your productivity to others. Many of these older salespeople relish seeing you become distressed. It is called *cracking a green pea*. Work underground. Share very little of your business with other salespeople. Keep your business to yourself. Do not share your goals with others. Practice mini self-rewards. Find reasons to do good things for yourself and others. Practice giving to people in key areas of your job. I found chocolate worked real well with the people in the office. They would always accuse me of trying to bribe them and I always admitted they were right, but when it came time to get help, they would always be there for me. It **never** hurts to be nice.

Sales Momentum

Well, you have done all the right things, and sure enough, you just completed your first sale. Heads turn and your manager and fellow salespeople wait to see if you are just a flash in the pan or if you have a real big family (as in, what will happen when his uncles and cousins run out), is a joke you will often hear. But, your success continues and you have begun to believe you might just have a career here. **Be careful.**

What is *momentum*? Momentum happens when people are at a certain confidence level in their own minds. Some of the new people will have it because by working with the basics, success will come naturally. Sometimes this momentum is called beginner's luck because we see that the initial surge falls off in a couple of months. The loss of momentum is caused by the salesperson taking his eyes off the ball. These new salespeople also pick up bad habits and take shortcuts. This loss of momentum can be avoided if the salesperson takes his business seriously and continues to practice the basics.

Momentum is a mental urge that works best in an uncluttered mind, a body full of energy and a not-so-serious, fun-loving heart. Momentum is a balloon that grows with each success. Momentum is a runaway train—forget the brakes. The best time to sell another car is immediately after you just sold one.

Avoid Power Drains

Each *no sale* will take some of your power away while each success will revitalize you. Learn **not** to let your highs be too high and learn **not** to let your lows be too low. The more you learn about your career, the more success you will have. As time rambles on, you will have the opportunity to step back and appreciate the overview.

At the early stage of your selling career, you should be careful not to hang out in the *dope rings*. (A *dope ring* is a group of salespeople (dopes) who gather during business hours to compare notes, tell jokes, and generally demoralize each other.) Avoid these crowds even if you find some of the high rollers in the ring. Many of the more experienced salespeople specialize in cracking rookies. Beginners are just jokes to them, and while these people are not really rotten to the core, they are not far from it.

> **A *get-me-done* is a person who has no credit, very little credit, or just bad credit.**

Be a lone wolf and work on the quiet. Keep to yourself most of the time; planning your day and making a list of things you will do when there is absolutely nothing to do. Imagine you are earning $72,000 per year and you are working 45 hours per week. Your monthly average income is $6,000. Your average hourly salary is $31.

The point of this exercise is to help you understand the value of how you must use each hour. Your income is based on you being involved in direct face-to-face negotiation for just a portion of the 45 hour week. The rest of that time is dedicated to studying the inventory, training, meetings, meals, stocking in trades, making calls, and any number of legitimate activities. All of these activities pay about $31 per hour—especially the empty do nothing hours. How many of these empty hours does the average person have?

Parkinson's Law says that "work expands so as to fill the time available for its completion." Figure out how to reduce these nonproductive times and you will automatically increase your income. Observe your productivity by keeping an eye on the clock. While most people clock watch because they are interested in when it is time to leave, you will be watching to see how much you can achieve before you must leave.

I was made painfully aware of this fact during the early part of my career. One Saturday morning I met a customer and after qualifying and demonstrating him we began to work the deal. The first warning sign (that I did not read) was that the guy was willing to do whatever I asked him to do. I learned later that this was the behavior displayed by a *get-*

me-done. (A get-me-done is a person who has no credit, very little credit, or just bad credit.) They will do whatever you ask because they need a car. I spent all that Saturday morning, and most of the afternoon, with this man. I refused to give up.

In the end we got him a car. I felt great until I looked at my commission. I had sold the car so cheap that the dealer only made enough profit to pay me the minimum of $50. The head desk man was a huge bear of a man. He called me over, got up from his desk and told me to follow him. We went outside and got in his car. He took off for the interstate.

For the next hour I learned the inner secrets of the car business. He was not gentle. He told me that there was only one reason we were taking the ride and that was because I showed potential. He explained that Saturday was the biggest day in a salesman's week and I had just blown the prime hours for $50. I started to get the point. He asked if I had a family. When I said yes, he asked how I was going to feed them on $50 per day. I did not have a good answer.

That was a real turning point in my career and I began to find out that I could still help customers win and also provide a decent income for my family. This business is just like any other business. If you work smart you will do well. Organize yourself and do not be a sheep. Follow your own lead. Every hour must be productive

More on Working Underground

When you work underground, it means you share very little of your business with other salespeople. You want to be congenial with your fellow salespeople, but keeping your business to yourself is very important. If you are keeping to yourself, then you will avoid many of the power drains that kill productivity. If you continue to have people who want to visit with you, it will be okay to do so if they will pay you your $31 per hour. If you must visit with someone then talk with a potential mentor who is earning $75 per hour.

Working underground involves keeping your cards close to your vest. Do not discuss the present or future details of your business with everyone. This type of action has the tendency to reduce your power.

Witness two salespeople having a conversation with their manager:

> "Hi, Mr. Manager, I have three parties coming in today and they are sure buyers."
>
> "That is good, Charlie, and what about you, Walt?"
>
> "Well, I need to call and firm up some appointments. I will get back to you."
>
> "Good enough, Walt."

All day the manager will be checking with Charlie.

Which of these guys is in the no fail position? Let your work speak for you and at the end of the month you will be looking at a pile of money Plan your work and execute your plan. Operate on a need-to-know only basis. Do not expose yourself to additional risk without having a good reason for it. Remember, one or two confidants tell only one or two more. How long will it take before everyone knows your business?

Daily Variation

Power is not constant in human beings. We have our ebbs and flows and ups and downs. In the life of a professional salesperson, you need to work with this variation in power. One guy compared this power variation to two scuba divers. One diver has two full tanks while the other has one full tank. Which one will be able to stay under longest? We are like these divers. But instead of tanks, we have minds.

Some days we are unstoppable and on others, the same tasks are just plain difficult. The unstoppable days are easy to deal with, but what about those down days? The days when your manager is completely unreasonable and everybody wants to get away from him, or the days when each customer is a problem or has an issue. The answer is to have a plan.

First of all, plan on these days coming quite often. Know that on some days you will be working with a one tank day. What can you do to be good to you? Take a long walk, have a great lunch, do something good for someone just because you can, pick a couple of people to cheer up, sell something. You can and should plan this list of things while you are hot and happy. Tuck it away—you will need it.

It is in the power of the mind that you will set the playing field for a more consistent power supply. Whatever affects the mind affects your power. How did you feel after the last heavy night out drinking? Did it affect your mind? How was your power? How did you feel after your last perfect date? How about the best night's sleep you have had in a long time? How about a good workout? How were your thoughts and your feelings?

Is there any wonder that good thoughts produce good feelings and when good thoughts and feelings combine, we have good results? Can we use this mechanism in sales? Learn the things that lift you up. What are you passionate about? Do you love sunsets? What do you really want? What is it that you are afraid to admit that you want? How did you feel the last time you made a big conquest? Is your mind free? Where are you headed? Who do you love? What is sacred? What makes you smile?

The human equation is not a simple one. All of the above issues affect our personal power. It is up to you to explore what lifts you up; salesmanship and life flow together. Since you cannot separate them you might as well have a great life and be a great salesperson.

Thoughts are Things

I remember when I was a very young boy living in a semi-rural setting in the Deep South. We would have many people coming by our house with their wares. There would be two or three of these characters per day stopping in front of our door. My sister and I would call out to our mother that the ice man (this guy sold blocks of ice for what we called an ice box), or the watermelon man, or the vegetable man, or the meat man, or the fish man had arrived. Sometimes Momma would buy something and other times she would look but not find the quality she wanted. Sometimes the price would be too high and after a discussion, she would walk away from the deal.

A good salesperson must view thoughts the same as Momma viewed the peddlers. Many thoughts will pass before you, but you do not have to buy into all of them. Be selective about what you buy into. Your mind is so important in selling that you cannot afford to be bogged down with negative thoughts that do not render a good return on your time investment. Chase away nonproductive thoughts and activities that do not replenish and sustain you.

In the old days, many prospectors would spend endless hours panning for gold. The method was simple: a stream carried many rocks and some gold downstream. The screen pan, or a sluice, caught rocks and other items and gold was kept while the worthless materials were discarded. Always be panning for gold. You will get a lot more rocks than gold. Know the difference. Remember your successes and observe the habits of those around you who are successful. Learn and retain all you can. Pick up what you can and implement what works. Push envy aside and ask your fellow salesperson about the details of a successful transaction. Most of them will be happy to share these thoughts with you.

Honesty and Integrity

Many studies of the top salespeople show that they are relentlessly honest. They are direct and their honesty becomes contagious. Before long the customer feels the honesty on an intuitive level and it is disarming. Honest selling traits are repetitive. Imagine an actor who practices the lines to one play and then performs that play every night. That performer will have less of a problem than one who has to learn new lines and play different roles each night. Honest people do not have to remember to cover up deceit. Even when the event is successful, there is less chance of repeat and referral sales because the liars do not trust themselves to fool the buyers several times. The effort is not there to pursue a continuing relationship.

Often drugs, alcohol, affairs, and poor health practices are typical of the dishonest salesperson's life. It is not a matter of being a good Christian, or Buddhist, or even a loyal partner. It has more to do with what works year in and year out. The job can be done with or without integrity and honesty, but only one leads you down the path of real success. The choice is yours.

> *"Nothing great was ever achieved without enthusiasm."*
>
> Ralph Waldo Emerson

Success

Move Fast

An early show of enthusiasm will reap great benefits with your manager. Be a high-energy person. High-energy people are winners. They have enthusiasm. Exhibit a high level of enthusiasm from day one; first impressions are important. Be alert and open-eyed. Keep your head high and shoulders up. Avoid hands in the pocket and folded arms. Soon others will say, "There is something special about that individual." They may not know what that special quality is, but other winners will immediately identify with it. They will unconsciously seek you out. Winners seek out other winners.

During World War II, the Germans perfected the art of desert warfare. They developed the tank into a force for defeating enemy forces in North Africa. Under Field Marshall Erwin Rommel, they enjoyed great successes against British and American forces. They were to meet their match in one U.S. General George Patton. One of Patton's firm beliefs was to move fast and never hold onto real estate. He believed in constantly advancing and making the enemy die for *his* country. Patton was a winner.

Selling automobiles has many of the same tenets as Patton's battle strategy. We deal with people who make decisions based on impulse 70-80% of the time. These customers will usually make a buying decision in the first three days. Because the buying decision takes place quickly, you will need to react quickly. At this point, we will assume the customer has been through your system and did not buy for whatever reason. You realize you must move fast, advance the deal and not hold onto real estate.

First, review the underlying causes as to why the customer left and then decide if there is any reason to call him back. If you see no reason to call him back, then devise an alternative plan to work with a partner. Give your information to your partner. See if a change of personality can do anything to close the deal. Your partner should be someone you feel good about working with.

Be ready to close.

What you have just done is to force yourself to really decide the worth of following up on this customer. What you also have done is to invite a fresh point of view for this customer. Caution here: Don't wait too long to make your turn—you only have 72 hours to close this deal.

Second, call back and thank the customer for his visit and discuss any new thoughts you have had. Continue to use enthusiasm while working with the customer. Have a smile on your face—it will be felt on the other end of the phone. You may even employ a visual aid that makes you think of positive things while you talk with him.

Third, share your honest feelings about the deal with your customer. Since he is no longer in your store, you may be able to express yourself differently than when you were face to face. Many times this use of total honesty will be just the thing to advance the transaction to a winning conclusion. If there is nothing there, then move on!

Strike while the iron is **hot** In the Old West, the blacksmith would heat the iron red hot and then hit it while it was soft enough to shape. When the iron cooled, the opportunity to work with it would have passed. Know what you can do before you call back. Be ready to close. Don't push but help your customer solve his problem. Put your cards on the table. The idea is to move quickly. If you wait for a week to phone him back, you will generally be too late.

Your customer is ready to be closed. He has other things to do. If he still says no, re-close by making a mini-review of the situation. At the end of this mini-review ask the question: Before we end our conversation, can you tell me what I have missed? When the real hot button appears, use this opportunity to find a contingency that will work for everyone. Make the close and button it up immediately.

Talent, Hard Work and Success

If you see others closing deals and you are not having much success, do not let it bother you. This may be easier said than done. Often you will find those around who are no smarter than you and have no more experience than you do, but time after time, they end up with the deal and you go home empty handed. As a beginner, your confidence will be tried and uncertain. This type of situation can crack you and wash you out of the business before you even get started. Have a plan and work that plan. If you are observing others too much you may find that you are not busy enough working your plan. Remember that when you are driving down the road it is okay to glance in the rear view mirror, but if those glances turn into more than that you may find yourself in a car wreck.

How do you deal with selling jealousy? Perhaps a quote from George Gershwin can shed some light. George had been a long-time admirer of a very beautiful woman. An acquaintance told him, "that she had gotten married to someone else."

"If I wasn't so busy," he replied, "I would be upset."

Keep busy. Keep your mind on your job. If you are reading this book, then you are well ahead of most in the car sales business, and that may be just enough to lead you to success.

We use our ears to hear and our brains to listen.

A few people find they are just natural at this selling game. They are strong and consistent and earn huge amounts of money. Most are not as fortunate. This is where the training, discipline, organization, and preparation pay off. This is your career if you wish it to be. You can go anywhere from here, but you must invest in yourself. You must be a self-starter and you must be able to ignore the bad habits of others.

To close deals, you will have to train yourself to listen.

As in any new job, you will need to learn the basics and then relearn them. Most customers will not have a problem when you let them know that you are a new salesperson. Some people are more comfortable because they may feel that you are less likely to take advantage of them. I once knew a salesman who had been in the business for 30 years. He would always tell his customers he was a green pea. He felt this gave him an edge and even put the customer at ease. He did a lot of laughing with his customers—they had fun.

You will not actually be exaggerating when you tell your customers you are new. In many cases, they will attempt to help you. Do not pretend to be a know it all. If you are not cognizant of a fact, then do not guess. Admit you are still learning. Find the right answer and get back to them. We have all had to start a new job at some point in our lives and your customers will relate to that.

Have some fun, but know when to stop and get down to business. I had a real good friend who was so funny that he could almost have made it as a standup comedian. He would have them rolling at the closing table, but his closing rate stunk. After he entertained them, they would be ready to leave. They were still laughing when they left, but they were not driving a new vehicle and he had not earned a commission.

To close deals, you will have to train yourself to listen. Most of us are not good listeners because we have never been taught to do so According to a 1982 study of public school classrooms, "students get 12 years of formal training in writing, six to eight years in reading, one to two years in speaking, and from zero to one-half year in listening," though listening is perhaps the tool we use most in life[5]. Listening is a quality that we can become better at in the same way we learn any other skill. We must practice it.

We must learn hearing and listening are not the same. We use our ears to hear and our brains to listen. Active listening is difficult because we listen at between 100-200 words per minute and we think at more than 1,000 words per minute. We must make a deliberate effort to stop thinking what we will say next and let the customer know we are listening by making eye contact, nodding our head, taking a few notes, and repeating what has been said. When your prospect recognizes you

---

[5]ERIC clearing house on reading and communication skill, 1988, Hysop, Nancy B.; Tone, Bruce; ERIC identifier ED2951132

have listened effectively, they will feel appreciated and understood. After we have demonstrated we are able listeners, we will have earned the right to be heard.

It is great to get into a new field and to find out that you have a multitude of natural abilities, but you can do just as well as the natural salesperson if you apply and organize yourself. It may take you a little longer but the success will be just as satisfying. Do not give up!

Success without Enslavement

We must be committed to our work if we are to be completely successful, but like all good things in life, we must balance work with mental, emotional, spiritual, and physical needs in order to enjoy it all. The temptation to make more money by staying at work longer is something to guard against.

Many of you may have the need to prove yourself in other ways than making money. If you were fired on the last job, or not treated fairly, you may have a need to show you are still competent and useful. Some of you have huge expenses and you may feel the need to keep up your standard of living.

Warning: This is no time to overcompensate. Pace yourself.

Guard against spending too much time at the job because you love the success. The success is a lot better when you balance it with the rest of your life.

In summary, very few of us are natural salespeople. Again, most of us have to work hard at it. Many mistakes will be made before you can claim competence. Keep your chin up and know there are millions of men and women just like you. They are doing this job everyday and they earn a good living sticking to the basics and working their plan.

Goal Setting and Rewarding Success

Any good program that speaks about success will emphasize setting realistic goals. Most of us are not opposed to this idea; however, writing out the goal is where the problem usually begins. You may think you can just keep it all in your head, but it won't be effective. You must establish a written goal. You must not only write out your goals, but you must review them each day. Writing down your goal forces you to be clear and definitive and written goals have a much better chance of being fulfilled.

Goal setting is addictive if you tie rewards to them.

While there are many types of goals, what I am referring to here are dollar goals. What is the **minimum** dollar goal for your household? Making a simple budget is important to setting this goal. Keep in mind this is the minimum amount of funds needed to keep you going. I call this my *gotta do* goal.

The next written goal is my *wanna do* goal. This goal is usually set by gauging experience, the inventory, the pay plan, the mental and physical situation, and anything else that can be factored in. This is the big, but realistic number that you set for yourself.

This goal is better set as dollars than units. You cannot spend units at the grocery store. If your organization wants your unit goal anyway, then figure out the average income you earn per car. Divide your dollar goal by that average to determine your unit goal (example: $ goal = $4,200, unit $ average = $300, you need to sell 14 units). It is important to set realistic and measurable goals because if they are not correctly set you will abandon the practice, and that is not good.

Plan your goal setting before the next month begins.

Goal setting is addictive if you tie rewards to them. This is referred to as rewarding success. Rewarding success involves attaching something of value to your goal. This tactic inspires extra effort. Rewarding success is not a new idea. Even as young children we are introduced to rewards by our parents, schools, and even our peers. Do not wait for your dealer to set goals for you. Do it yourself. Think of something you feel strong about. It can be for you or for others.

Make an agreement that if you reach your goal you will perform the reward. Examine your feelings and react to what turns you on the most.

When you tie a real strong feeling to a goal, it will pull that goal along like a team of sled dogs. Before you know it, you will be half way toward achieving your objective and you might even find yourself raising your goal.

When the goal is achieved, do what you said you would do. Reward yourself as agreed and really enjoy it. This practice of attaching rewards to success is empowering. Avoid delays—act as soon as possible. Doing so will have a crescendo effect on your next goal-setting routine. Plan your goal setting before the next month begins if you can. Get into the habit of making your goal-setting plan at the same time each month.

Vacations

Some of the best times you will ever experience will happen on vacations. The French, Germans, and Italians take twice the vacation time as the average American. We are so work oriented that we let ourselves believe we can't get away, or that we can't afford it. We promise ourselves that we will take a vacation next year. You are beginning a new career and you will be told that after a year you will get a week or two off. If you can't wait that long, put a day off and a weekend together and get out of town.

Many salespeople will take the vacation pay awarded by their company and just keep on working. **You need the time off** and your significant other(s) needs the time off. There are other salespeople who do take the time off and even a little more. There is nothing wrong with paying for your own time if you are making good money. Remember the old adage that "rested horses win races."

Your Business within a Business

You can achieve anything if you know where you are and where you want to go. Do you want to give rise to your own business? Participating in a commissioned sales job requires many of the same tenets as running your own company. Take baby steps while operating inside an established business. It is a great angle to take to establish your own enterprise. You can use this time to save money in a 401K, and after a period of time, start your own business. Buy a house, condo, or other property. Establish equity so you can use it to borrow against if you need it to keep the business going. It is always easier to work with your own money.

Manage expenses and anticipate the unexpected.

There are plenty of people willing to loan it to you if you will pay back 20 cents on the dollar. If you start out with the right attitude, you could go from being employed to employing others within two to five years. If having your own business is important, you may find that working on commission helps you acclimate to risk taking. As a commissioned salesperson, there is never a set amount of money to count on. When you make a good budget, you will end up changing it to reflect new trends. It is also this way in business.

You will need to manage expenses and anticipate the unexpected the same as you do in business. You must develop a customer following, do follow-up, generate referrals, account for money, manage your time, develop long-term goals, advertise, and educate yourself. These are all business requirements, practice them here and they will come naturally if you decide to enter into your own business later in life.

The career paths from the automobile business are endless. Working in the dealership as a commissioned salesperson can be a great career if done right. There is less pressure and stress than being in management and the money can be great. There have been plenty of people who have become managers of all types including owners of their own dealerships and broker houses.

The paths can also lead to positions in the finance service industry, selling jobs of any type, positions with the manufacturer, service managers, and owners of service facilities. The list goes on, but it started with just a regular position on the front-line. Grow where you are planted.

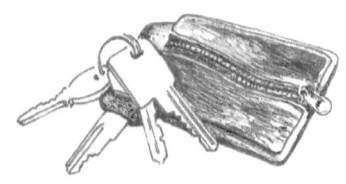

> "A man who dares to waste one hour of life has not discovered the value of life."
> Charles Darwin

Time Management and Organization

How much can you get done in a fixed amount of time? If you are organized and focused you will surprise yourself and others around you. I knew a salesman in the fleet department who would appear to be doing nothing at all and would have four or five cars out by noon. Now there are many super salesmen who can do the same numbers, but to do it without breathing hard adds to the magic. When asked how he did it so consistently he would say, "I know what I have to do, I know the steps, I have my system set up and I just do it." He also came in at 5:00 AM.

There is no doubt that having the ability to organize your day will make you a great deal of money. What are some things that you can do to reduce time spent?

Dead Time

One of the major drains on your time investment is not recognizing dead time. To recognize dead time you have to know what it is. How you define it is a very personal thing. Are you doing what you need to be doing to sell a vehicle? If you are not doing that then you need to take a good look at yourself. Keep busy. If there is nothing going on then get ready for the next sale. Make sure your sales folders are prepared. Review the inventory and make your calls. Realize that you make your money even when you are not with a customer.

Be prepared. Be disciplined. Be focused.

While you can never manage time itself you can manage how you use it or how you waste it. Be aware that another one of the leading drains is a failure to recognize and handle duplication. I noticed that many good salespeople failed to have tools. When they had a trade-in they would go around asking someone to loan them a screwdriver to take off license plates. They wasted plenty of time doing this and also lost money during busy times because they could not finish the transaction in a timely manner.

The greater sin was that they did it again and again. Ask yourself what task you consistently repeat. How can you reduce the total time spent to a more acceptable duration? Have a place for everything and have everything in its place. Know where it is. When you know where everything will be that you need you will build greater confidence in yourself and it will improve your closing ability as well.

Daily Book

Use a daily sheet. A daily sheet can be a single sheet of paper representing a day of the month that you place in a notebook – your *daily book*. **Trust nothing to memory**. Write everything down. Check the daily book each day. Keep at least three months of pages in the book. Keep one month ahead, one for the current month, and notes from last month.

If you want to be really organized you can buy an organizer or day planner from a local bookstore or office supply store. Many businessmen have years of these. It is amazing how things repeat themselves about the same time each year.

The back of each page can become a to-do list area. This area can serve as a place to prioritize your tasks. Divide tasks into things that you have to, want to, and ought to do. Carry forward unfinished tasks to the next day.

There is no defense against procrastination and lack of will power. If you can get into the habit of writing things down, this good habit will make you money and reduce your stress.

Sales Notebook

Notebooks worked well for me. One of the best notebooks for me was the one that I kept my sales records in. After each completed sale you will retain a copy of the buyer's order. Without fail, make sure to get this copy in your notebook. If you're busy, just stick it in an area of the notebook where it can easily be found later. Do not put it in your pocket or your desk drawer. If you place it in the same place each time you will be able to find it at the end of your work day. This effort requires a little investment of time, but the rewards are immense.

Be a self-starter.

This notebook is also a great place to put your commission slips. When the accounting office completes your deal you will receive a commission voucher stating the amount of your pay. You should already have a note made as to what your commission was; immediately compare these notes to what your commission slip now shows.

Do not wait until payday to resolve any differences. On payday all of the salespeople will be trying to get differences resolved and there will be mass confusion. Be a self-starter and depend on no one to keep up with your compensation.

Balance is Crucial

The keyword is balance. Observe those around you who seem to have a handle on life; find out their secrets for coping. Reduce stress by slowing down, organize your work, avoid toxic personalities, don't take things personally, be willing to forgive and let go of things, get professional clerical assistance.

Set your plan up daily and work your plan.

Do it right!

Time Management Aides

- Avoid duplications
- Develop good habits
- Have a place for everything
- Write it all down
- Prioritize
- Avoid procrastination

- Handle paperwork once
- Make dead time productive
- Plan your work and work your plan
- Keep good records

"Knowing is not enough; we must apply. Willing is not enough; we must do."
Johann Wolfgang von Goethe

Product Knowledge

Let's talk a little about information. In your new job the first information you will deal with is company policy. What do they expect from you? You will sign a pay plan and promise to follow company procedure. Then you will deal with product knowledge. How important is product knowledge?

Many companies will try to justify that they place a heavy emphasize on product knowledge because they hold weekly training sessions, but most of the meeting is about things other than training. Hardly any job is lost because one does not know the product. Most of your managers will not press you because they do not know as much about the product as the front-line sales pros. They succeeded because they knew how to make a profit. Most stores will expect you to acquire this skill on your own. There will be no real pressure for you to do anything in most used car stores, except to get results or get lost.

Walk the inventory.

Where do you begin? In new franchise stores there will be more emphasis on product knowledge and you will want to walk the inventory and see exactly what they have. Why is this important? Because it represents your best chance to make a commission.

If there is no inventory, there is little chance for a sale. Identify your top three lines and begin right away learning about each model in those lines. Do not wait until the next day or next week because that will never come. Do not go looking for spec books because hardly anyone will know where they are, and even if you do find them, you may not be able to carry them home. Start with the brochures or go online.

You want to know as much about the product as the customer does and those two areas are where most people get their information. A good way to increase your reading time is to cut down on watching television. Watch your favorite show, but turn off the TV between shows. Set a timer for a short period of time and read until it goes off. It pays to rise early as this is a powerful time to read and retain what you have read because you are fresher at this time of the day.

Establish a reading list and buy the book before you have the time to read it. If you have extensive drive time, buy the CD or tape and put it in your vehicle. Place items in the restroom—all jokes aside, this can be quality reading time.

Emotion leads to closes

Why be informed? We want to be able to talk intelligently with the customer. There is a lot of information on the Internet, so we must assume that our customers are using it to narrow their choices. When they reach our organizations, they have amassed considerable data. If the customer begins to realize they know more about your product than you do, then you may lose face and your sale.

On the flip side, you do not need to inundate the prospect with your product knowledge.

When you meet your prospect, you will automatically begin to get an idea of what he wants. This is known as finding hot buttons. Make your presentation an outline. At each major heading you will be looking for any body language or other sign of interest that informs you where you should stop to spend more time. Dwell on these intense interest areas and recall to repeat them at any point in the transaction.

Hot buttons are the things people care about the most. For some it might be the radio, other may crave big tires. It is usually very easy to figure out what these hot buttons are. It gets a little more complicated when the vehicle is for more than
one person.

What you are really trying to do with your presentation is to increase the emotion. High interest areas are all about emotion. Emotion leads to closes and that is why you should instinctively search for these gems. What do you touch on when you work a hot button? Validation, empathy, respect, and an ability to listen are just a few. You will also be appreciated for not wasting the customer's time.

> *"There is more credit and s atisfaction in being a first-rate truck driver than a tenth-rate executive."*
> B. C. Forbes

Truck Sales

The first vehicle that I ever drove was an old Ford two-ton truck converted to haul pulpwood. One day out of the blue my old man said, "Get in there and pull that truck up boy." I told him that I did not know how to drive. He said, "'bout time you learn then." With instructions that sounded more like grunts and groans, he and Dan Junior, his hired hand, got me going. I was ten years old.

Owning your own pulpwood truck gave one the status of boss. If you owned two to three trucks then you were considered to be doing very well. The truck was everything. It was our shelter in the Florida storms, it was our payload mover, and it was our way home. If the truck broke down, chances were you would not see anyone to hitch with since we were usually several miles back in the forest. We learned a lot about how to make the truck go no matter what the circumstance.

Regardless of their application you must know how to recommend the right vehicle.

Today's small business owner faces similar circumstances. He depends on his equipment just as we did. Most of these people own between one and four vehicles. Your job is to qualify them for the right vehicle. Review the chapter on ***Qualification*** and remember to question, question, and question.

Are you hauling or towing, what is the weight of your load, do you need space more than payload capacity, where do you operate your vehicle, how much do you tow, what fuel economy do you expect, how long have you been in business, how is your credit, and what can you afford? Putting your businessman into the right vehicle will bring you repeat and referral activity.

Another segment of the truck market is the casual and recreational user. This segment is huge and represents greater profits and commissions than just about any other segment of the automobile business. Dealers have an opportunity to finance larger sums for longer periods of times, sell accessories, add to parts and service businesses, because trucks are retained much longer past the warranty coverage periods than for car customers. These buyers are more interested in towing than payload capacity.

> **Two-wheel drive pickups have push power at the rear wheels, while four-wheel drives add pulling power at the front axle.**

Regardless of their application you must know how to recommend the right vehicle. Until you are sure about the applications, please turn the deal to more qualified personnel when you feel that you are in over your head. This is not the place to bluff your way through. You must know the right answer. Let's review the basics.

Pickup trucks carry six people (payload) and are used to tow. Crew cabs can carry as many as six people. Payload is how much weight the truck can safely carry. Towing is how much weight the truck is rated to pull.

Pickups come in compact and light duty or heavy duty versions. Compact trucks are popular because fuel prices are higher today. Full-size pickups equipped for light duty use are among the largest sellers of all trucks. They serve as much for general transportation as they do for working issues. These pickups are called half-ton pickups. Heavy-duty trucks are used for big work jobs. These heavy duty trucks are also called three-quarter-ton, one-ton, and one-ton plus.

Pickups are constructed as two-wheel drive and four-wheel drive machines. Two-wheel drive pickups have push power at the rear wheels, while four-wheel drives add pulling power at the front axle.

Pickups are built in three basic cab styles: regular cab, extended cab and double cabs (often called crew cabs). These cab styles have come about because trucks have expanded from being used for business reasons to also being used for family and recreational reasons. Today's pickup trucks can be almost as luxurious as many top of the line cars.

Pickups can be purchased in several trim levels: basic, nicely-appointed, and luxury level models. Basic level trucks assume rough work will be done and consequently may have vinyl seats, rubber mats, manual windows, and few creature comforts. Nicely appointed units may have nearly everything in them except for leather seats, sunroofs, backup cameras, navigation systems, over-the-top sound systems, rear entertainment systems, etc. Most of these latter items will be standard or readily available on the luxury models.

The three factors that influence towing the most are the engine, transmission, and the rear end.

Ratings of half-ton, three-quarter-ton, and one-ton are the trucks you will usually be dealing with. Originally the half-ton truck was able to carry about 1,000 pounds of people and/or cargo, but we find this to be an outdated notion today. Most Ford F150s, Chevy 1500s, and Dodge 1500s are able to carry between 1,500 to 2,000 pounds. The three-quarter-ton truck can carry up to 4,700 pounds and one-tons can, in some cases, carry up to 6,000 pounds. Be sure to consult the specification charts when dealing with payload requirements.

An area of opportunity for you will be with people who confuse payload with towing capacity. Most will believe that a one-ton truck will out-tow a three-quarter-ton truck. Remember that *payload* is what the rig will carry and *towing* is what it will pull.

The three factors that influence towing the most are the engine, transmission, and the rear end. Every pound that is loaded onto the truck must be taken away from the towing capacity, thus a crew cab and a regular cab with the same power train (the motor transmission and rear end) will tow different weights.

Which will have the highest tow rate? The regular cab will tow the most because it weighs less. The two-wheel drive will tow more than the four-wheel drive. Since towing will be the biggest single demand from your recreational users, be sure to have your charts readily available to show them. When the information is in writing it has a great deal more legitimacy and believability than by simply stating it.

SUVs, Vans and Chassis

The truck category also contains SUVs, mini and cargo vans, and chassis cabs.

Special utility vehicles are very popular. Their ability to tow heavy loads and seat several people is their greatest asset. In most instances these vehicles have the ability to go off road. They will have four-wheel drive in most cases. They have tremendous ground clearance to avoid becoming high centered. Their engines are strong and the rear ends are geared low so they can negotiate steep terrain, heavy mud and snow, and move heavy loads from a stop up to cruising speeds. These machines are traction monsters. They do offer the opportunity for great recreational moments in areas where other vehicles would be ill equipped to go. They also offer greater protection in collisions.

Some of the downsides of SUVs are that they are not fuel efficient and they are expensive. SUVs are also top heavy, which causes them to be more prone to roll over. Finally, their traction advantage in inclement weather can cause overconfidence in the driver and lead to not allowing enough time to brake properly.

Minivans are the replacements for the old family station wagon. They are people carriers most of the time. Many models are available as all wheel drive (AWD); however, the front-wheel models are usually enough for most situations. They are designed with low-entry heights making them user friendly for very young and senior users. The minivan does multiple tasks because the seats can usually be adapted to provide a flat floor. In this mode it can be a weatherproof cargo mover.

Cargo vans differ very little from minivans in that many minivans are down-sized versions of the cargo van. These vans all have one mission in mind: to be cargo movers first and people movers second. Your customer will often be concerned about how much weight the van can carry. Vans are usually rated the same as pickups. The major categories will be one-half, three-quarter, and one-ton vans. Creature comforts are usually not very important in this type of vehicle.

Chassis cabs and van bodies are incomplete vehicles. They are manufactured to be completed at the local level. Body converters are abundant. Your dealer will have a relationship with many of the converters. The chassis cab usually consists of the cab and has rails for bodies to be attached. Other chassis types allow for a vast array of bodies to be added by conversion companies (or skilled individuals).

"If you believe in yourself and have dedication and pride - and never quit, you'll be a winner. The price of victory is high but so are the rewards."
Paul Bryant

Daily Spiffs

Many selling organizations offer spiff programs. A *spiff* is a small bonus paid directly to a salesperson. One type of spiff is called a C.I.F., which stands for *cash in fist*. This type of incentive is meant to reward the salesperson right away with cold cash on the spot. When this money is paid at the time of the sale it becomes an extremely powerful motivational tool. If management does not act quickly as promised, then the affect can be reversed just as quickly.

Payment in greenbacks is more effective than check or vouchers. Some dealers will allow you to have your proceeds put in your paycheck, because many salespeople are afraid they will spend the cash in a nonproductive manner. I always figured that the money was better off in my hands than someone else. These CIF's are paid out for many reasons; such as, *hat tricks* (three deals sold in one day), volume bonuses, selling old stockers, selling specific colors, surplus models, holiday awards, etc.

In addition to daily spiffs there can be week-long and month-long awards. Most of these spiffs are announced at the beginning of the month and serve as incentive to lower employee turnover, increase overall productivity, and maintain interest over the long haul. The employee is generally paid these spiffs at the sales meeting. Your dealer wants every salesperson to see how much money is being paid out; he wants you to be excited and earn more money for both you and the company.

Limit the Cash You Carry

There is a lot of money around the car business. Many times you may be paid several hundred dollars in spiffs and cash-in-fist awards. Most salespeople carry this money around, but I recommend as soon as you receive it that you take it to the bank. You should not wait until the end of your shift because you will forget about it and a lot of money burns a hole in your pocket.

The hunger factor.

If your bank is a long distance from work then open up a second account nearby. You should; however, allow yourself a small amount of pocket change as a personal reward for doing such a good job. But, many times, at the end of the pay period, salespeople will receive very little money in their paychecks because they received a great deal of cash awards, which no taxes had been withheld. On payday, when those taxes are withheld, there are often a lot of unhappy faces. This area of money management is easily controlled if you bank your spiffs immediately.

Another advantage to having a small amount of money in your pocket is the hunger factor. Somehow carrying small cash reserves always helped me to drive a little harder on every deal. A bunch of cash in your pocket can cause you to lie back and become too comfortable. You will also be better able to resist making loans to people who might never pay you back.

"The best leads are those that are referred to you by satisfied customers."
Scott Kramnick

Referrals

What is the best advertising in the world? The very best advertising is word of mouth. The cost is almost nothing and the return comes in the highest form. It is no wonder that companies, large and small, covet referral business. When you work hard to take care of your customer or account, there will always be a positive return. People will want to do business with you. The car business has had a poor reputation in many circles. People are afraid of car dealers but they must have transportation, so when they find a good person to deal with, they will value your integrity. Think of how you feel about the person who does your hair, your dentist, your minister, etc. You return to these people because they do a good job for you.

How Do You Increase Referral Business?

Build the foundation first. The foundation for getting is giving. Give your customer a good show. Make it an event to be remembered. Take a picture of them and their new ride. Many people feel that they can take shortcuts to getting good referrals, but the real secret to getting good referrals comes with hard work. You must do a good job of selling the product first.

How does this translate into selling automobiles? A salesperson using this tactic must know the product well enough to give the customer the right advice. His intention must be to truly help. He must have high self-esteem so as to be able to offer the same to his buyers. His sales presentation must be professional and informative each and every time. The presentation must not be overdone or underdone. The customer must feel the empathy. If all of this is reasonably accomplished, the stage is set for the next step.

> **Most of your referrals will send you people who are just like them.**

Ask for the referral. Now that a sound business relationship has been formed and your people truly like you, and the service has been great, they'll want to tip you. But how do you tip a car salesman? You help them by telling them you'd like a good referral. A good referral is someone who you will enjoy working with as much as you have enjoyed working with these customers.

But, hold on for just a moment. Suppose you really did not enjoy working with those people? What if you hope you never see them again because they were the biggest pains you have ever met? I always felt that I may not have had any control over meeting them the first time, but I sure could and would control the next meeting.

Most of your referrals will send you people who are just like them. The good ones I wanted, but there were many that I put into my files with a note to never contact. I also never asked them for a referral. My theory was that I was mining for gold, not rocks and pebbles. What that really means is that after many years of prospecting and building a referral base I expected to see quality people returning to me most of the time. I was not disappointed for choosing quality over quantity. Each year my clientele got better and my job got easier.

There are a couple of areas of discussion when it is best to ask for the referral. Some feel that you should ask for it immediately after delivery as you say good-bye. Others feel that it is best to let a little time go by. I used both approaches. Right before saying good-bye the customer might mention the subject of referrals first; all I had to do was thank them and let them know that their referrals to me would be welcomed. If they said nothing, I would briefly mention that I would appreciate them telling any of their friends and relatives about me and our dealership. Then I would follow-up with a thank you card, followed by a phone call well before the first week ended.

The purpose of the call was to thank my customers once again for their business, and to ask if their friends approved of their new vehicle. The conversation that followed allowed several places to discuss referrals. I also used periodic written follow-ups to allow my customers to know that I was still at that dealership (or if I had moved to a new dealership). Regardless of the overall message there was always an implied request for referrals.

When you work referrals ask who sent them in.

Asking for referrals when you have not done the job of selling is like asking for a paycheck when you have not done the work. Even when the job has been done well, hitting the subject of referrals too hard or having poor timing can have an adverse effect.

Another area of controversy in the referral arena is whether you should pay for them or not. I have no moral issue with paying for referrals. It is done in many places and by many people. It is also considered illegal and unethical by many. Some organizations that I have worked for used this method with good results. I also have offered customers incentive to send others to me. I found that many very satisfied customers told me they would send people my way, but only because they wanted them to be treated well. I stopped offering incentives and my referral percentage increased. In my final years selling at a dealership, the percent of repeat and referral business went as high as 87% two years in a row.

Finally, when you work referrals ask who sent them in. Praise that person in the referral's presence. Praise the original customer again somewhere before your transaction ends. The referral process is like a giant chain letter: one person tells another and on and on it goes. When you praise the previous link in the chain, the next link will expect the same praise when they send someone to you. It paves a way for excellence that they will wish to participate in.

Again, do not overdo this simple practice as people will begin to question your intentions. I also discovered that by paying for referrals to the first link in the chain then person number two often began to question person one's motive. No one wants to feel that they may have been used. Once I knew who had sent this person in I could quickly look back at the original transaction, to see what amount of profit I had made, and have a good idea of how this deal needed to be worked in case persons one and two compared notes.

The final act in the referral loop was to make a call or drop a note to "old Fred" and thank him again for sending in another great customer. Many times those "old Freds" would remind me of exactly how many people they had sent and I would always tell them they were going to get a great deal on their next vehicle, and they always did. Keep that chain going.

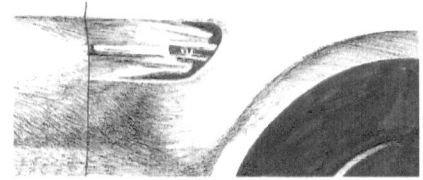

> *"Technology is like a fish.
> The longer it stays on the shelf,
> the less desirable it becomes."*
> Andrew Heller

The Value of Using Technology

It seems only a few years ago that a fellow salesman and I were having a big discussion about the computer. He was a little older than I and had vowed to never get involved with this new technology. Just a few days later he had a meeting with the owner of the dealership. During their conversation he stated his position rather forcefully. He was a very good salesman and was shocked when he was told that he could either learn to use the computer or leave. He learned the computer.

Many of us have resistance to new technology, but it is good for us to continue to learn. My eighty-one-year-old father-in-law did a 180° turnaround with technology in less than a year. When we tried to convince him how wonderful our computer was he just could not see how one would benefit him. Now he has two and uses them every day.

The computer is the bare minimum in the modern technology arena.

For a car salesman there needs to be a computer somewhere in his home, at work, or both places. If possible, get a laptop, too. If you do not have the time to do the input then pay someone to do it for you. I found that the kids loved to make a few bucks entering my sales record into the computer. The computer is the bare minimum in the modern technology arena. Then there is the cell phone, the PDA or Blackberry, the iPhone, the mini PC, and an endless array of items that allow you to keep in touch and store data.

While the technology is available at very affordable prices you must provide the will to learn and use it. Adapting to these new devices will bring you success and you will make more money because they will help you make better use of your time. Just make sure to learn how to use your devices; read your instruction manuals or, if necessary, call on your kid's assistance. I also found it rewarding to have a reliable computer expert to assist when all else failed. The cost is nominal and they will do house calls.

*"Eat to please thyself,
but dress to please others."*
Benjamin Franklin

Dress Neatly

Many dealers will allow a dressed-down approach. The idea of removing the shirt, tie, and sport coat began back in the 1950s with dress down Fridays. Many companies used it as a reward and employees enjoyed the break from the routine. The car business has benefited from this practice because many of the employees wore loud and inappropriate attire. The practice was so widely held until the non-endearing term of "dressed like a used car salesman" emerged. Today dress-down Friday has become a full six- or seven-day exercise by many stores. Public opinion seems to be okay with the new full-time concept. Be prepared to pay for the clothing yourself unless your company is unusually generous.

> **Shoes will be the most important article of clothing in your wardrobe.**

Whatever program you find yourself participating in, be sure to keep your apparel clean and wrinkle free. Buy enough clothes so that you can have clean reserves. It is always a good idea to have a change of clothing in your vehicle or office drawer due to unanticipated events.

I always found head gear to be advantageous. During hot days I was more comfortable in the sun and when it was cold I lost less warmth through my head. Hats and caps are usually allowed at most stores.

Sunglasses are great for reducing glare, but unfortunately, it perpetuates the old stigma of the automobile salesman as the slick guy behind dark glasses. Many regarded the practice as hiding shady intentions or a more gangster type of visual misnomer. Since most car lots have very little shade, a good pair of sunglasses is more than a fashion statement or an attempt to hide your soul from customers. I found that a good compromise softened the impact of wearing sunglasses. My approach was to initially meet the customer without the glasses. After several moments I would ask the customer if they minded if I could don my shades. I never had anyone say no.

Shoes will be the most important article of clothing in your wardrobe. You have read several times in this book how important comfort is in selling automobiles. Remember that comfort starts with you and becomes contagious to your customers. The right shoe can make all the difference in how comfortable you are during your workday. Choosing the right shoe starts with placing comfort ahead of style. When purchasing the shoe, remember that your feet are not the same size. Determine which foot is bigger and buy the shoe for that foot. Do not be misled to believe that the shoe will stretch after you break it in.

This job can involve a lot of standing. If you begin to experience pain that goes up the leg to the back, it is probably coming from your shoes. Insoles can help. Try the over-the-counter type, and if necessary, pay a visit to a podiatrist. If you work in areas where you receive snow, buy yourself a good pair of boots. The difference between a good pair and the bargain type is usually only about $30. It is important to keep your feet warm, dry, and to have good traction, so take the plunge and buy a quality boot.

> *"The three great essentials to achieve anything worthwhile are, first, hard work; second, stick-to-itiveness; third, common sense."*
> Thomas Edison

Do It Right and Do It Now

Okay. Now you have surveyed the lay of the land. You know a lot more about what you are getting into than you did before. Yet, there is still that doubt, and those nagging questions: How will I do? Can I really pull this off?

Relax, you will do just fine. Enjoy yourself and if you do not like the first store, try another one. There are a lot of styles and approaches in the automobile industry. You will not be perfect but you will get better every day. Apply yourself and follow the tips I have showed in this book.

Likeability also starts at home.

Selling is something that we all do every day. You will be meeting people who are looking for a friend. Some of them will be afraid of you and others will want a fair treatment. This is about meeting people. You have been meeting people all your life. Now you will be paid for it and you will probably be paid very well.

One of the fringe benefits of being able to sell automobiles is that you get to meet the entire cross section of the population. You will become an observer of people. You will become a quick study of people. You will know more about a person in one hour than their next door neighbor has come to know in five years.

You will not be selling them a product though—you will be selling yourself. One of the secrets to selling yourself is to really like you. Do you look to others for acceptance? Then stop and look to you. What do you want? What makes you happy will probably make others happy too, but pleasing other people is not your main concern.

That may seem egotistical, but you have heard that charity starts at home and then spreads abroad. Likeability also starts at home. Others can feel when you are comfortable with yourself. There is that word again: comfort. Comfort is the best friend you can have in sales. When you like yourself it reflects in how you dress, how you walk, the cheerfulness in your voice, you have a special look in your eyes, you smile a lot, you are on a mission, you are calm and confident, and you want something good out of life.

Keep it simple, take it one step at a time and enjoy the ride.

Good Luck.

About the Author

John E. Woullard was born in Hattiesburg, Mississippi on February 16, 1948. Married to wife Gaye for 29 years; they have three sons. John currently lives in Denver, Colorado and enjoys the Rocky Mountain experience.

John attended Stetson University in DeLand, Florida, and after graduating in 1970 was hired by Sears. He attended Sears National Training Academy for nine months. After assignments in Savannah, Georgia and Auburn, Alabama, John was promoted to the Sears Tower in Chicago, Illinois as assistant sales manager of the hardware department.

After spending five years with Sears, John relocated to Denver where he served in many store management positions with Montgomery Ward and Target. John's on the job experience prepared him in the art of merchandising to the demands of the public. Tours as operation manager prepared him to handle people, payroll, budgets and expense control.

After spending 15 years in the retail business, John entered the automobile business as a green salesperson. His front-line experience was delightfully new and provided a great income. He was promoted to sales manager and later went into fleet sales.

After John's experience in dealerships, he opened his own dealership named Wheelsworth, Inc. and specializes in brokering, consulting and consignment. John also owns a real estate company, and training aid known as The Automobile Sales Training Institute of America.

For the last 24 years John has been in direct contact with the automobile buying public. He now shares his vast selling experience with you.

Read the book and you'll know that John does not believe in short cuts. He does believe in preparation and that to be the best you must practice at a high level. By doing so, you will prepare yourself for a fun and profitable career in sales.

Glossary

ACV: Actual Cash Value

AWD: All wheel drive is a type of four wheel drive that allows the power of the vehicle to reach all four wheels. It differs from standard four wheel drives in that it can be used on dry pavement and usually cannot be disengaged.

Be back system: An organization that recognizes that not all customers will buy on their first visit. There is great care used to reduce closing pressure so that the customer will possibly return and buy from them.

Bell to Bell: Schedules that forced the employee to work from store opening to close (i.e. 8 am to 8 pm).

Body building: When a truck has a specialized body added to fit the specifications of a custom user. Some typical bodies are flat beds, dump beds, cube boxes, stake beds, wrecker bodies, etc.

Burn through ups: Describes the actions of a salesperson that engages a customer (up) and does not follow the steps of the sale. The major transgression here is that the salesperson does not get the customer to go on a demonstration ride or turn the customer properly.

C.I.F. This is a type of *spiff*. It stands for *cash in fist* and is handed out very close to the performance of a completed task in green backs. It is a powerful motivating tool.

Cap cost reduction: Capitalized cost reduction is any amount (cash down payment, trade in credits, rebates or other credits) of money that reduces the amount being financed. In a regular loan it is called down payment.

Close: The transition from a prospect who is considering a purchase to one where the prospect has made to decision to buy.

Closer: An employee who is designated as a person who regularly goes in on a deal to bring it to a profitable close.

Control Room/Sales Tower: The dealer normally employs managers to administrate the flow of each deal; these people general are found in a location known as the sales tower or control room.

Cracking rookies: The behavior of senior salespeople who tease, frighten, and destroy their esprit de corps when they are down and or mislead green salespeople because they enjoy seeing others suffer. They make a job out of trying to make these beginners quit the job.

Crew cabs: Pickups that have seat belts to accommodate five or six people.

Demo ride: A demonstration ride is a step of the selling process where a customer is taken for a drive in vehicle that they are considering. Its intent is to acquaint the customer with the performance capabilities of the vehicle.

Dinosaur-style stores: These are the stores who embrace tactics typically used in the 1960 through the late 1980 period. These years typified the era of rip offs, lies, misrepresentation and outrageous behavior towards customers.

Dope rings: A group of salespeople who form a group and engage in conversation. Most store management frown on these rings because they do not present a good image to customers.

Four squares: A method of presenting a deal to the customer that involves the management dividing a piece of paper into four squares where the sections are labeled trade, payment, selling price and down payment. Figures relating to the proposal are entered into the squares and the salesperson works to find the part that is of the most interest to his party.

Get-me-done: Customers who have bad, limited or no credit will usually do almost anything that they are asked because they need a vehicle; hence they are called *get-me-done* because their primary mission is to just get financed. The terms and type of vehicle are not the main concern.

Hat tricks: Three vehicles sold in one day.

High rollers: People who make a lot of money.

Holdback award: *Dealer holdback* is a dollar amount that usually amounts to about 2-3% of the dealers invoice or MSRP. This money is usually held by the manufacture to an agreed time (usually once a quarter). These funds assist the dealer in paying expenses to show and advertise its inventory.

Hot buttons: A very keen interest of the prospect in a specific item or function of the vehicle. This area of extreme interest is something the customer feels he cannot live without.

In the box: Describes what happens when the customer is taken to the finance office. The finance office is known as "the box" because there is one way in and one way out of the room.

Inking: Another word for signing a contract or any other document.

Kick it: If a trade in is causing a problem in the closing of a deal manager will seek to "kick it." This term simply means to exclude the trade.

Lemon law: American state laws that help customers with vehicles that have had a lot of problems. These vehicles must have repeatedly failed standards of performance and quality. Lemon is the term given to vehicles that fall into this high failure rate category.

Loading the salesman's lip: A manager's instruction to a salesman as to specifics things he is to say or do to his prospect.

Married: Situations where two people are destined to share equally in a deal if it can be brought to a successful close.

Money cost: The fee for use of money over time known as interest.

MSRP: Manufacturer Suggested Retail Price. The idea of this pricing methodology is to standardize pricing for all regions, but to still allow for marketing variations.

One-second lane change: A road maneuver that simulates what a driver may have to do in an emergency lane change situation. It is designed to demonstrate the sure footedness of a vehicle.

Orphaned owners: Customers who have purchased from a dealership in the past and their original salesperson is no longer with the company.

Payload: The weight of cargo. The rating of a vehicle's payload generally means how much the rig can carry. Some of the factors that allow for payload variation are frame thickness, springs, tires, wheels and other suspension elements. When calculating payload, one must be concerned with the downward effect of gravity resulting from the cargo, people and any (other none standard) equipment added to the vehicle.

Pop ups: Customers who, when insulted or offended in some way, will stand up abruptly and indicate that they are about to leave.

Power train: The term power train and drive train mean the same thing. The items that most often make up the power train are the engine, transmission, driveshaft, differentials and wheels (also propellers or tracks).

Putting the customer out: The manner in which your organization allowed the customer to leave.

Referrals: A mode of marketing that depends on word of mouth, for getting new customers.

Residual: The amount that remains after an automobile has been used for a specific time or after an amount of miles have been inflicted on it. It is used here to represent values referred to in leasing situation (i.e. a vehicle whose MSRP is $30,000 as has a residual of 60 percent after two years will have a dollar amount of $18,000 as its residual worth).

Sales Tower/Control Room: The dealer normally employs managers to administrate the flow of each deal; these people general are found in a location known as the sales tower or control room.

Security deposit: Security deposits are one time refundable payments made at the inception of a lease to guarantee coverage of good condition at lease end.

Skater: A salesperson who knowingly steals a customer from one of his fellow salespeople.

Spec books: The specification book and refers to manuals sent from the manufacturer that gives data to every model in the lineup.

Spiffs: A small bonus that is paid to a salesperson for selling a specific item within a specific time. Spiffs are usually paid by the employer or the manufacturer.

Table a deal: The actions the salesperson makes when bringing the transaction to a point where the negotiation goes on paper for the purpose of presenting this proposition to management.

Turns: Sales maneuvers that involve a second or third party coming in to address a customer so as to close a deal that will improve the dealer's position.

Unit: A single vehicle.

Work underground: A person who does not reveal very much about himself and how he/she does business. They keep to themselves and their profile is low.

Index

$5,000 rule 34
Actual Cash Value. *See* A.C.V.
A.C.V. 18
advertising 16, 20, 23, 89
appraisal card 17
appraiser 18
arbitration 45
AWD 84, 101
be back system 52, 101
budget 33, 43, 50, 72, 74
business cards 53, 57
cap cost reduction 51
cash in fist. *See* C.I.F.
chassis cabs 25, 84
C.I.F. 87, 101
close 8, 9, 14, 15, 30, 31, 32, 33, 34, 35, 36, 37, 38, 40, 41, 42, 43, 44, 45, 47, 49, 52, 63, 68, 69, 70, 76, 101, 103, 105
commission 10, 32, 45, 63, 70, 74, 77, 79
crew cabs 82
daily book 76
daily sheet 76
decision maker 33, 35
desk manager 1, 2, 18
education 2, 8
equity 49, 74
experience 1, 2, 5, 9, 10, 13, 16, 22, 25, 26, 27, 28, 37, 45, 47, 69, 72, 73, 96, 99
F & I manager 24
finance 8, 16, 23, 24, 48, 49, 51, 74, 82, 103
General Sales Manager. *See* GSM
green peas 44
GSM 15, 16, 23
honesty 2, 66, 68
hot buttons 30, 36, 80
income 2, 10, 36, 47, 62, 63, 72, 99

insurance 8, 17, 24
inventory 16, 20, 21, 22, 23, 60, 62, 72, 75, 79, 102
Kicking the trade 18
lease 49, 50, 51, 52, 104
lot lizards 11
magnets 57
Manufacturer Suggested Retail Price. *See* MSRP
minivans 84
MSRP 51, 102, 103, 104
negotiation 1, 17, 38, 44, 62, 104
organization 3, 8, 42, 69, 72, 101, 104
organizations 2, 18, 23, 25, 36, 52, 80, 87, 91
paperwork 20, 24, 44, 46, 47, 60, 78
personal space 27
pickups 82, 84
power train 83, 104
presentation 30, 35, 36, 37, 42, 44, 46, 53, 80, 89
productivity 7, 28, 48, 60, 62, 63, 87
proposal 13, 14, 15, 102
prospect 12, 13, 14, 21, 31, 33, 36, 37, 42, 43, 49, 50, 51, 52, 55, 56, 57, 70, 80, 101, 103
prospecting 55, 58, 90
push power 82
qualification 32, 33
referrals 40, 53, 55, 74, 89, 90, 91
reward 72, 87, 88, 95
salary 7, 10, 16, 62
sales department 22, 57
sales hawk 15
sales tower 1, 13, 14, 46, 102, 104
security deposit 51
skater 22
spiff 23, 87, 101

SUV 84
taxes 49, 50, 88
tools 42, 48, 56, 75
tower manager 13, 14, 15, 16, 20, 21
towing 41, 42, 81, 82, 83
transmission 17, 21, 83, 104
turns 9, 72
used car 16, 17, 18, 20, 45, 79, 95
used car department 16
veteran 10, 13, 32, 46
visualization 59
warranty 50, 51, 82

MC²Books
McGrew Group
3207 S Geneva St
Denver, CO 80231
Voice: +1 720 282 3129
Fax: +1 720 282 3129
Email: designs@mcgrewgroup.com
URL: www.mc2books.com

For more information on this title or other titles from Mc², please visit us at mc2books.com!

Other titles available from MC²Books available now include:

Critial Mass: A Primer for Living with the Future
by P.C. McGrew & W.D. McDaniel

Designing a Document Strategy
by Kevin Crane

Wrestling Legacy Data to the Web and Beyond: Practical Solutions for Managers and Technicians
by P.C. McGrew & W.D. McDaniel

Want to be an author? Visit mc2books.com for more information.

www.ingramcontent.com/pod-product-compliance
Lightning Source LLC
Chambersburg PA
CBHW021145230426
43667CB00005B/267